Over Simon Bryant's 25-year career, he has cooked in Thai, Indian and award-winning fine-dining restaurants including the Hilton Adelaide, where he was Executive Chef for seven years. From 2006 to 2009, he co-hosted 152 episodes of ABC's *The Cook and the Chef* with Maggie Beer. Simon is now Creative Director of the food and wine festival Tasting Australia. He is also a providore of single-origin, traceable, non-GM foods and a semi-competent vegie gardener.

Simon is a passionate promoter of ethical food issues, including paying fair prices to producers, the use of native Australian foods and the treatment of animals. He is an ambassador for the Animal Welfare League, Animals Asia Foundation, Oxfam fair and GROW, and Meat Free Week, among others.

Vegetables, Grains and Other Good Stuff is the follow-up to Simon's bestselling debut, *Vegies*.

VEGETABLES, GRAINS
& Other Good Stuff

SIMON BRYANT

PHOTOGRAPHY BY ALAN BENSON

LANTERN

an imprint of
PENGUIN BOOKS

INTRODUCTION

I'll start with confession: I don't believe what you choose to eat is
a world-shattering, completely defining characteristic of who you are.
Frankly, I am grateful for food, period. When so many less fortunate
people go to bed hungry, it seems a little indulgent to bang on the way
we do about this or that dislike, dietary preference or culinary craze.

It is my job to cook and I love it. Yes, I am slightly obsessed with food, but
I endeavour to keep my fanaticism in check. I believe everyone has the
right to choose what they eat, be it for reasons of religion, ethics or health.
However, my food preferences are just that: *preferences*. I am mindful that
if someone cooks for me, it's a nice thing. I was brought up to be grateful
for the offerings at the table, whatever they are. For this reason, I will
accept your hospitality and eat as your custom dictates and generally finish
whatever is on my plate and be genuinely thankful. I guess if you had to
stick a label on my head, it would read 'situational flexitarian'.

I don't believe in diets. In my opinion, we all know what to eat. If it's fresh,
free from numbers, fairly unmolested and something that societies have
relied upon for centuries, it's probably okay. And it's going to let you know
you're on the right track because you will feel okay. It's that simple.

Professionally, I have access to just about any food under the sun. I'm a chef
and we are food dealers. We make phone calls in the wee hours of the night,
we drive miles down dusty tracks to meet people who don't speak much but
have what we want. We rendezvous in dark loading docks and hand over
wads of cash to dodgy-looking people for the good gear. We have even been
known to get up early in the morning (heaven forbid) to get first dibs at the
markets. Some of these ingredients – the vegies, grains and other good stuff –
I squirrel away for my own cooking at home. And this is what I cook.

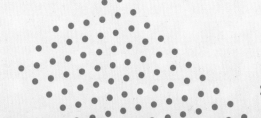

INGREDIENTS

PULSES

Otherwise known as lentils, beans and peas, and chickpeas. The variety of lentil usually refers to the colour of the inside seed, which is confusing because red lentils can look brown if they are unhulled (skin on). Even more confusingly, some black lentils (like the black gram) are so-called even though the seed is white. The variety can also refer to the strain of lentil seed. For example, the Puy lentil is a flecked blue-green lentil cultivated in Le Puy, France. We grow this seed rather well here too, and I am a huge fan of our Australian version (called French-style green lentils in this book). Chickpeas are classified by the origin of the seed: the larger Afghani kabuli (garbanzo) or the smaller, more fibrous Indian desi. Pulses can also be unhulled or hulled (skin off) and/or split. If a hulled lentil, chickpea or pea is split, it is referred to as a dal. Confused? Wait, there's more. Certain dals are often referred to by their Indian names. For example, masoor dal, which is split red lentils. I have tried to be as specific as possible in these recipes to avoid scrambling your mind!

Anyway. Lentils are magical and I encourage you to seek out a local, single-origin (i.e. one farmer's crop, not a mish-mash of appellations thrown together) lentil before you declare them 'hippy food'. It's also good to know that lentils have a season, just like fruit and veg. They do taste better fresh, so try and seek out recent harvests. Over time, the skins start to degrade and their aroma may also become tainted if they sit in storage for too long, leaving them with a distinct dusty smell. Lentils are also a great water-wise crop, which makes them ideal for our climate. Our growers now have lots of different varieties on the market, so if you ate Australian lentils a decade ago and were underwhelmed, please go back and give them another shot. Things have come a long way in recent years. As a final note in celebration of lentils, unlike most forms of protein, they do not require refrigeration during transportation, which makes them an excellent choice if you are concerned about the associated environmental costs.

Like their legume cousins, beans tick many environmental boxes. They are also playing a part in the new dietary frontier of gut health, which many believe can influence a range of health conditions. This is because beans that are soaked, cooked and cooled (and reheated again if you choose) are a great source of resistant starch (RS), which has been touted as a 'superfood' for the digestive system. You'll no doubt be hearing a lot more about this topic in the next few years, but here's a quick explanation, without all the science blah. RS passes through the small intestine undigested; it is instead broken down in the large intestine and feeds the good bacteria down there. This process produces a fatty acid that not only fuels the body but keeps lower intestinal cells healthy – which in turn may provide protection against cancer. This is huge news, but all you really need to know is that beans are excellent for your health, and full of flavour and substance.

Unlike lentils, dried beans and chickpeas need a soak before cooking. Overnight is best. Use plenty of water: four to five times the volume of water to pulses. I always soak pulses in the fridge during the warmer months. Their protein level makes them subject to spoilage; you'll notice a little fizziness in the water if this happens, so it's best to throw them out and start again. Always discard the soaking water and use fresh water for cooking. An insoluble carbohydrate leaches out during soaking so the pulses are far more digestible if the water is discarded. If you forget to soak overnight, a cheat's method is a hot soak. It's not ideal, but it will do. Simply bring the pulse up to a simmer in four or five times its volume of cold water, then pop a lid on, turn off the heat and leave to soak for 3 hours. Discard the soaking water and proceed as usual. There is a certain train of thought that salted cooking water toughens the skin on pulses but I find it plays very little on the end result. And don't forget chana dal is a chickpea, not a lentil, so you need to soak it!

GRAINS

If you are a paleo person stop reading now, because – call me neolithic – I believe in grains for all sorts of reasons. They have copped a ton of flak recently, but don't believe the hype. I sympathise with people suffering from coeliac disease. I couldn't fathom a life without really good bread. I am a firm believer that the so-called advances in agricultural strains of wheat, baking methods and refining processes have a lot to answer for. If you have a genetic predisposition to coeliac disease and your small intestinal filli have been bombarded and inflamed with gluten proteins, they are now flat and angry, so you can stop reading. If, however, you just feel a bit bloated, tired and uncomfortable after stuffing down a white-bread sarnie, don't throw the baby out with the bath water and declare all gluten your enemy. Ask yourself how whole civilisations were built and sustained, fuelled by the 'staff of life', if everyone was sleepy and windy after eating the daily staple?

Minimally processed, stoneground wholegrains are nutritional powerhouses. Over-refining of the whole grain, steel-cut milling, additives, bread improvers (oxymoron if ever there was one) and bleaching are modern developments. Real bread features none of the above and you might just be able to thrive on it as part of a balanced diet. The deal-breaker for me is slow, natural wild yeast fermentation over days, which breaks the glutens and makes them readily digestible. One more thing. Just because bread is labelled as sourdough or artisan doesn't mean it is free from all the no no's above. Real bread has flour, sourdough culture, salt, water and maybe some honey or oil: that's it. Grrrrrr!

Highly refined durum wheat is okay for a treat, but mixing it up with other grasses and grains, such as spelt and rye, freekeh and bulgar, polenta and pearl barley, is going to make you feel a lot better. There are so many options available nowadays you could literally go a season without eating the same grain twice.

Freekeh, young green wheat that is traditionally burnt or commercially roasted at extreme dry heats, is available whole or cracked. It is often tolerated by people who have minor issues with gluten. Bulgar (burghul wheat), whole-grain wheat kernels with the germ and bran intact, can be fine, medium or coarse-ground. Barley is one of the oldest cultivated grains. Pearl barley has its outer hull and bran removed, while barley groats are whole.

Rice is nice; yup, it is and I often hanker for good old white rice. Just treat it, like white flour, as a 'now and again' thing, rather than a go-to staple. Basmati rice is very low-GI, so if you are eating white it's a good option. Look for the really long-grained variety. The best stuff is aged so that the starches diminish giving it its characteristic non-clingy finish. You may have to ask your Indian grocer for it, as aged basmati is often guarded behind the counter! When cooking jasmine rice, be mindful that new-crop rice will always end up gluggier and so will need a good wash. After paddy rotation, the new crop will have higher starches because the paddy is rested and soil nutrients are therefore more available. It's a little variance in harvest that can throw you if it is not on your cooking radar.

Wild rice is a grass and a 'cousin' of the Asian rice species. I love the texture of the tough little husks and the chewy centres. The flavour itself is something I can never really put my finger on. I just like it. Wild rice takes a good 45 minutes to cook, which can be expedited by soaking for a few hours but I never do. I find it softens the outer husks too much and I like these to stay on the grain, then cook until they are just bursting.

As a final note, it is environmentally controversial growing rice in a water-poor country like Australia. Rain-grown rice may sound a little fancy, but if you care about the Murray Darling system, you should look out for it.

PSEUDO-CEREALS

'Ancient grains' seems to be a catch-all for any grasses, seeds, etc, walking the catwalk of food coolness at the moment, certainly for those card-carrying wholefoodanistas. Endless pursuit for the new periodically takes us back to the old. The pseudo-cereals quinoa and amaranth are now viable crops for our farmers: established crops of quinoa in Tasmania and numerous trial crops in Western Australia are bringing good yields and exceptional products to our markets and amaranth also looks promising. It was thought at first that our low altitudes may not be conducive to quinoa, a South American native, but it's all working out, which is very good news for a number of reasons, not least because food transportation costs and emissions are lowered if we keep our tables brimming with local produce. Also, god knows our farmers need some wins with crops that make them price makers not takers.

The issue not often discussed is that when food trends are created in the west, it can devastate poorer economies overseas. But, you may ask, what's the problem if farmers in Peru are seeing unparalleled demand for their toil? Well, this demand does push up the price but the farmers don't always reap the benefits; the middle men are the real winners. Secondly, the situation can get so severe that the local population can't access their own traditional staple, as black marketeering and speculative hoarding may occur. The answer? It would help if the food industry didn't behave like the tween fashion industry. These blips in popularity can create real issues for farmers who have crops that are now 'uncool'. When chardonnay became a cliched beverage, no one stopped to think about the vintners with established vines and no real market for their product. I'm not trying to be the food fun police but I'm just sayin' there are consequences to our frivolity. In the case of quinoa, either buy local or consider paying for a fair-trade overseas product. I know this labelling scheme isn't perfect but at least it is trying to get some cash back into farmers' communities.

Quinoa is a great source of protein and is gluten-free, so I guess all the fuss is not surprising. The distinctions in seed colour – red, brown and white – don't greatly alter the flavour or outcome of a dish so I consider them interchangeable. There is however a difference between quinoa seeds and flakes: the latter produces a sticky porridge texture when cooked. Quinoa seeds need a quick but decent soak to remove the saponins, a bitter-tasting component naturally occurring in the plant. Amaranth seed is a great source of magnesium, protein, calcium and dietary fibre, and is gluten-free. It doesn't require soaking and it cooks in less than 20 mins; however, my favourite way to prepare it is popped (see page 12)! If I am simmering the seed, I always use the absorption method and leave it slightly al dente.

Buckwheat, despite its name, isn't a wheat at all. The seeds are a fairly complete protein and it's another super-quick cook with no soaking required. I like the random-shaped seeds, which look like little groats, and their nutty, earthy flavour and slightly chewy texture. Soba is the Japanese term for buckwheat, and the soba noodle is just that. Many soba noodles contain a high proportion of another flour, usually wheat, however, so it's worth checking the ingredients for 100 per cent buckwheat.

NON-WHEAT FLOURS

I use a number of non-wheat flours including rice, tapioca, chickpea (besan) and lupin. They really are not hard to get, with most being available at Asian grocers. I am a firm believer in spending more time getting the ingredients right and less time cooking so I never begrudge this 'hunter gatherer' time. It's all part of the adventure. I find wandering supermarket aisles completely soul-destroying and alienating, but being greeted by a grocer or market stallholder with my name and a smile is one of my favourite parts of the day!

SOY STUFF

Many recipes in this book use firm, silken firm and silken tofu – think of textures descending from Swiss cheese to junket, and you get the idea! All types are readily available nowadays. I also like using tofu that has been frozen, thawed and crumbled. I have no idea what happens to the proteins in tofu when it's frozen, but when it's then thawed and crumbled, it takes on a mince-like texture. What's more, a ton of water is extracted when it thaws and this allows the tofu suck up loads of flavour during cooking. Give it a go.

In this book, I also use various beancurd skins and sticks, by-products of the tofu-making process. These soy goodies are made from the film that rises to the top when the soybeans are boiled. When the film is dried and used whole, it's known as beancurd sheets (or skin); when dried, folded and rolled, beancurd sticks. You'll find them at the fancier Asian grocers.

For the beancurd sheets, I like the large fresh stuff that is sold frozen. Alternatively, there are folded-up, shelf-stable sheets that resemble an A4 pad of semi-translucent paper. They are drier than the fresh sheets, so require a thorough moistening before use to prevent them from cracking. Beancurd sticks come in various shapes and thicknesses, from firm, flattened tubes to crumbly pieces. You'll find them in the dried goods section of Asian grocers. The regular dried sticks are large, fragile and fawn-coloured, while sweet beancurd sticks are caramel brown, sturdy and flat, a bit like old-fashioned chewing gum. They have a lovely chewy texture once rehydrated. The crumbly beancurd pieces look a little like discarded shopping bags left too long in the sun! They are brittle and slightly yellow, and pretty much turn to dust if you grab them too firmly.

I also love smoked tofu. You don't need any fancy equipment to smoke. Just make a fire, put it out, enclose the food over it, give it 10 mins and – bingo. The cheapest and best way is grab a wok with a lid and a wire insert. If you want to use the wok for cooking afterwards, line it with foil before adding your smoking mix but as the smokiness can still permeate the steel, I have a dedicated one. Then pop in a handful of untreated wood chips, a couple of spoonfuls of rice (to retard the burning) and whatever woody aromatics you like (tea, star anise, pepper, dried mandarin peel, cinnamon). Adding a tablespoon of brown sugar to a smoking mix will give a nice deep-brown burnish to the finished product. Or you can leave the aromatics out and just go for pure smoke. Regardless, do it outside or under a very good extractor fan! Fire the wok up to get it smoldering over constant low heat (or let it catch fire, kill the flame and allow it to burn out). Pop some drained and pressed tofu in, cover with a lid and let the smoke go to work. I usually just use my fire pit and pop whatever I am smoking on a grill plate when the fire is dying, and chuck the smoking ingredients on the coals and smack a lid on top to trap a little smoke. It's not an exact science: just have a mess around with whatever method suits you.

NUTS AND SEEDS

Nuts and seeds bring amazing flavour and crunch to dishes, and are of course a great source of protein for vegos. I eagerly await new-season nuts in autumn, as the oil content is high and the taste amazing. (Rancidity is best tackled by storing nuts in the fridge.) I use lots of peanuts in Asian dishes and absolutely love them, especially the sensational Queensland-grown redskin. I buy them by the ton – literally: I get them cold-pressed to make an authentic peanut oil for higher-temp frying. That's how much I love them!

SEAWEED

In Australia, we now have some exploratory licences for harvesting native seaweeds but the industry is still in its infancy. And as the seaweed plays such a vital role as shelter and breeding grounds for our ocean life, I commend Primary Industries for erring on the side of caution when ascertaining whether they can be harvested for consumption.

Wakame, however, is an introduced invasive species, so if you are eating the Tasmanian product, you are not only eating from some of the freshest water in the world but helping weed the ocean as well. Win! Wakame is the king of seaweeds with a rare combination of stunning ocean flavour and a 'just chewy enough' texture. The harvest is scant in the colder months but it is generally sold fresh and frozen (my pick) or dehydrated, so availability year-round is no problem.

Kombu and other robust seaweeds are used mainly for flavouring rice and soups or for their natural agar content, which brings body to stocks. They are then generally discarded after cooking. Nori is on the gentle end of the seaweed spectrum. This farmed red algae is minced and dried using a process similar to making paper and is sold in sheets, as well as in flakes.

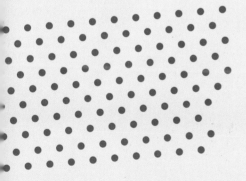

DRIED MUSHROOMS AND OTHER 'WEIRD' STUFF

I would really like to publish a book showing white people's faces as they try to navigate the dried goods' section of Asian supermarkets. Don't worry, I used to be one of you: juggling seventeen different packets (and dropping them continually), arguing with your shopping partner and trying to decipher the label while holding a recipe that demands a certain weird ingredient and generally looking like a kid whose mum forgot to pick them up from school. Yes, I have come home with dried jellyfish when I wanted white cloud fungus; but the dog liked the jellyfish and I learnt the grocer's name and slowly worked up the courage to ask a few questions.

Here's a quick 101 of dried mushrooms and fungus. Shiitakes are the king of Asian mushrooms for texture and flavour. When reconstituted from dried, they take on a pleasant slippery, rubbery texture. (Fresh shiitakes, however, are a treat when you are after a slightly chewiness and robust flavour.) Wood fungus is so-named because it grows on wood! It's thick (like dried tangerine peel) and black, with some white on one side. It is sometimes sold in strips. Cloud ear is black but thinner and lighter than wood fungus. It is also a little frilly around the edges. White fungus is a delicate, paler version of the above. Black moss is a lichen, which when dried resembles teeny, coarse cellophane noodles. To help you out we've included some pics and a detailed rundown of other dried stuff in the Hot pot recipe on page 195, as it contains an excessive combination! Set aside some time to explore this mysterious and challenging corner of the Asian grocers and you will be rewarded. ◗

Asparagus, zucchini AND haloumi WITH quinoa AND popped amaranth

½ cup (95 g) white quinoa
(see Ingredients)

salt flakes and cracked
black pepper

250 g haloumi, cut into
5 mm thick slices

½ cup (125 ml) extra virgin
olive oil

2 zucchini (courgettes), 1 green
and 1 yellow if available,
sliced into long ribbons

2 bunches asparagus, trimmed

juice and grated zest of 2 lemons

¼ cup (50 g) amaranth
(see Ingredients)

250 g cherry tomatoes,
some halved, some quartered

8 zucchini flowers, torn (optional)

½ bunch flat-leaf parsley,
leaves picked

½ bunch mint, leaves picked
and torn

I have always been accused of too much aggression with my heat when cooking – nearly all my mentors have asked me to calm down. It's a symptom of starting my career over Asian wok burners, which have around four times the power of a domestic hob's flame. It's made me impatient and to this day I have trouble using weedy little flames and gently sauteing vegies. So chargrilling delicate new-season asparagus and zucchini is probably a food crime, but I love it. You run the grill at full-tilt but the tr ick is to work quickly, exploiting the smokiness, then get the stuff off asap so it keeps its crunch. You need plenty of oil to conduct the heat: the tell-tale dark lines will be testament to this.

The haloumi, on the other hand, contains enough natural fat to facilitate cooking without any oil. Oiling the cheese gives a less charred, more melted finish, which is not what I'm after. However, without oil you run the risk of the cheese sticking to the pan and unless you have a very sharp, thin spatula, you may just leave the grill marks behind. Lining the pan with baking paper is a great wayto prevent this. Popping amaranth is a kitchen task that reminds me how simple things can amaze. I pop a smile when I see the little seed instantly double in size. Have a lid handy if you don't own a dust-buster: the amaranth can get a little enthusiastic and launch itself all over the room.

1 Soak the quinoa in water for 30 minutes, then rinse well. Place in a saucepan with 1 cup (250 ml) of water. Cover and bring to the boil, then simmer for 5 minutes. Remove the lid and simmer for a further 5 minutes. Remove from the heat and leave for 5 minutes, or until the quinoa unravels and most of the water has absorbed. Drain, then season and set aside.

2 Heat a chargrill pan or heavy-based frying pan over medium–high heat and line with baking paper. Grill the haloumi for about 3 minutes each side until charred. Leave to cool, then rip up. Lightly oil and season the zucchini and asparagus. Remove the bakign paper from the pan and cook for 1–2 minutes each side until charred. Set aside. Place the remaining olive oil in a screw-top jar and add the lemon juice, salt and pepper. Shake until well combined.

3 Preheat a large heavy-based frying pan with a lid over medium–high heat. Chuck in the amaranth, cover and shake vigorously for a couple of minutes (as with popcorn). Once the popping subsides, tip the amaranth into a bowl.

4 Divide the quinoa among plates and drizzle with dressing. Add the haloumi, zucchini and asparagus. Scatter with tomatoes and zucchini flowers, if using. Drizzle with a little more dressing, then sprinkle with popped amaranth, lemon zest, parsley and mint. Season with salt and pepper, and serve. ●

Green garlic <u>AND</u> spinach soup <u>WITH</u> tarator

6 bulbs (about 240 g) green garlic, with 10 cm stems

¼ cup (60 ml) extra virgin olive oil

2 teaspoons salt flakes

200 g baby spinach

Tarator

3 slices white bread

120 g walnuts

150 ml extra virgin olive oil, plus extra for drizzling

1 teaspoon salt flakes

2 tablespoons lemon juice

1 teaspoon red wine vinegar

This soup is a recent addition to my repertoire. The hero is the green garlic, which delivers all the thrill of eating tons of garlic but without the social repercussions. Green garlic is just immature garlic, comprising a single bulb (as no clustering of bulbs has yet formed), a sweet stem and edible skin. You will see it in the garden before the heat starts to mature the garlic; it looks like a spring onion with a bulbous base. In this recipe, the tarator tempers the garlic with its smooth nuttiness, while also working to baffle (in a friendly way) the intense greenness of the soup.

1 For the tarator, soak the bread in ½ cup (125 ml) of water for 5 minutes, then gently squeeze it dry. Using a mortar and pestle or a food processor, pound or pulse the bread, walnuts, olive oil and salt to the consistency of chunky peanut butter, then fold in the lemon juice and vinegar.

2 Peel the garlic to remove the tough outer layers, then nip off any little roots at the base. Chop the stem into 2 cm lengths and cut the bulb in half.

3 Heat the olive oil in a saucepan over medium heat. Sweat the garlic for 5 minutes or until soft, then add 1 litre of water and the salt. Bring to a simmer for 3 minutes, then fold in the spinach, using tongs to push it under the water. Remove from the heat after 30 seconds and use a stick blender to puree until smooth.

4 Divide the soup among bowls and dollop a couple of tablespoons of the tarator on top. Finish with a drizzle of extra virgin olive oil. This soup is also delicious cold. ●)

Barbecued corn cobs WITH chilli mayo AND parmesan

4 corn cobs, in their husks

⅓ cup (100 g) Egg yolk
mayonnaise (see Basics)
or good-quality bought mayo

½ teaspoon chipotle chilli powder
or 2 tablespoons chipotle
in adobo sauce

grated zest of 1 lime

handful of coriander leaves,
finely chopped

salt flakes and cracked
black pepper

⅓ cup (25 g) finely
grated parmesan

lime halves, to serve

Youngish, green-tinged corn husks are best for this recipe. Soaking the cobs before subjecting them to the barbecue stops them from burning, and also adds a little moisture to the already juicy kernels. By the end of cooking, the silks will be burnt and the corn will have just the right amount of charring dotted all over it. If the husks are brown and withered to start with, the dish will still work but not as well.

The chilli mayo is a great accompaniment but if you can't be bothered, you can just slather butter over the corn at the last minute. It's still great eating, and using any excuse to make smoke in the backyard is an Australian tradition of course, so this is essentially an act of patriotic reaffirmation. Gas barbies are fine, but I believe that wood and coal produce an infinitely better result – and on a clear, crisp spring evening there's nothing like sitting around a fire and dribbling food down your chin.

1 Submerge the corn cobs in water for 30 minutes, then drain and pat dry with paper towel.

2 Preheat a barbecue to medium–high.

3 In a small bowl, combine the mayonnaise, chilli, lime zest and half the coriander. Season with salt and pepper, and stir until well combined.

4 Place the corn cobs on the preheated barbecue and cook, turning every couple of minutes until charred all over. Turn the heat to low, then cover and cook for a further 10 minutes or until the corn is tender.

5 To serve the corn cobs, open up the husks and remove the silks. Brush with the chilli mayo, then sprinkle over the parmesan and remaining coriander. Serve with lime for squeezing over and extra mayo on the side. ●

Sesame, avocado AND cucumber rice balls

2½ cups (500 g) short-grain brown rice

2.5 cm dried kombu (see Ingredients)

⅓ cup (80 ml) rice vinegar

¼ cup (60 ml) sake

1 teaspoon salt flakes

1½ tablespoons caster sugar

1½ tablespoons toasted black sesame seeds

pickled ginger, to serve

light soy sauce, to serve

Filling

1 lebanese (small) cucumber, seeded and finely diced

1 large avocado, roughly mashed

¼ cup (40 g) pickled daikon (or cornichons), finely diced

1 tablespoon freshly grated horseradish or 2 teaspoons good-quality wasabi paste

½ teaspoon salt flakes

I know cucumbers are not yet at their best in spring but you won't notice in this dish; they are included here for crunch, along with the pickled daikon. Be mindful that the lurid yellow pickles sold in Asian supermarkets contain food colouring and often MSG and aspartame, which are three things I would rather do without. If this is the only option available, go for cornichons instead. On that note, real wasabi is not cartoon-frog green. Most of the pastes are full of numbers, and frankly I'd rather swallow a calculator. Instead, I always trim down the last of the winter's horseradish, wrap it up in plastic film and freeze it. If you are feeling flush though, you can buy some of our amazing Tasmanian (or New Zealand) wasabi, which can be ordered online and always arrives in tip-top shape.

Short-grain brown rice works brilliantly here. 'Real' sushi rice is incredibly smooth and starchy – you need to rinse it really well or you'll end up with a gluggy mess. There's no such need with brown rice because the starches are way more stable, plus it also has the added health benefits of the bran and germ. Win-win.

1 Place the rice and kombu in a bowl with 1.5 litres of cold water and soak for 10 minutes. Tip the rice, kombu and soaking water into a rice cooker or saucepan, then adjust the water so that it is about 2.5 cm above the rice. Bring to a simmer over high heat, then reduce the heat, cover with a tight-fitting lid and gently simmer for 40 minutes. Remove from the heat, take off the lid and leave to rest for 10 minutes. Turn out the rice into a 30 cm baking dish (about 5 cm deep), discarding the kombu.

2 In a small saucepan, combine the vinegar, sake, salt and sugar over low heat and stir until the sugar dissolves, without letting it boil. Add to the rice and gently fold through without breaking the grains. Cover with a tea towel.

3 For the filling, combine all the ingredients in a bowl. Take a 20 cm length of plastic film and spray lightly with water. Place 2 tablespoons of warm rice in the centre and create a round about 1 cm thick, then place 1 teaspoon of the filling mixture on top. Gather the edges of the plastic film and bring together to form a ball, then twist the top and compress gently. Undo the plastic film and reshape the ball with damp hands. Place on a baking tray and sprinkle with sesame seeds. Repeat with the remaining rice and filling, then place in the fridge for 30 minutes to firm up.

4 Serve the rice balls with pickled ginger and soy sauce for dipping. ◗

Spring pot au feu

3 globe artichokes

juice of ½ lemon

8 g dried porcini

2 bay leaves

8 black peppercorns

salt flakes

4 sprigs flat-leaf parsley

2 carrots, peeled and
cut into 3–4 cm lengths
(the yellow heirloom variety adds
a burst of vibrant spring colour)

2 baby leeks, white parts only,
cut into 3–4 cm lengths

2 parsnips, peeled and cut into
3–4 cm lengths

250 g waxy potatoes
(such as kipflers or bintjes),
cut into 3 cm chunks

3 small pearl or pickling onions
(or golden shallots), peeled

2 celery sticks, trimmed

1 bunch broccolini, trimmed

100 g green beans, trimmed

600 g fresh broad beans, in pods
(300 g when podded)

½ cup (80 g) fresh peas

5 sprigs thyme

4 sprigs oregano

⅓ cup (80 ml) extra virgin olive oil

grated zest of ½ lemon

cracked black pepper

cornichons, pickled onions,
horseradish or mustard,
and mayo, to serve

crusty bread, to serve

This dish is a great slap-it-down-and-let-people-go-nuts number and I love it. When artichokes, broad beans and peas are piled up in the market, I grab the lot and know exactly what I'm cooking for dinner. Drink the accompanying broth straight after a mouthful of artichoke and you'll experience that weird chemical reaction that artichoke sets off, that anything you eat directly afterwards tastes sweet. This is the reason wine people get so upset with dishes containing artichoke, but it's exactly the kind of food trick I love.

Good cooks understand the importance of good stocks and that doesn't mean the stuff out of a packet. Once a stock comes to a bubble, it is always just simmered; if you allow it to boil furiously it becomes cloudy, resulting in a very different taste. (This is especially true if the stock contains oil or fat, which then emulsifies through the broth.) If you simmer the stock gently in this recipe, you will be rewarded with a clear and clean flavour. Now you're probably searching the ingredients list for 'stock' and thinking it amiss, but the point is it's created from all the vegies gently imparting their flavours into the cooking water. Those spring vegies you're carting home contain a potential stock waiting to be unleashed. This is something for nothing and that's good cooking.

1 To prepare the artichokes, cut off the top third of the leaves, trimming the older outer leaves back until you see a very pale green–yellow patch on the base of the leaves. Scoop out the hairy choke from the centre, then nip the stem about 5 cm from the lowest leaves. I sometimes run a peeler down the stems if they look a little woody (as you would with old asparagus). Then just plonk the artichokes into a bowl of water with a squeeze of lemon juice to prevent them discolouring.

2 Fill a stockpot with 1.75 litres of water and add the artichokes, porcini, bay leaves, peppercorns, 1 tablespoon of salt and the parsley stems (saving the leaves for garnish, if you like). Add the carrot, leek, parsnip, potato and onions or shallots, and bring to the boil over medium heat. Turn the heat to low, then cover with a lid and simmer for 20 minutes.

3 Add the celery, broccolini, green beans, broad beans, peas, thyme and oregano, and simmer for about 5 minutes or until all the vegetables are tender but still hold their shape.

4 Remove the vegetables with a slotted spoon and arrange on plates. Drizzle with olive oil and sprinkle with lemon zest, salt and cracked pepper. Divide the broth among bowls.

5 Serve the vegetables with your choice of accompaniments (pickles, horseradish, mayo and so on) and the bowls of broth with crusty bread. ◗

Freekeh AND lentil tabbouleh

½ cup (100 g) unhulled red lentils
(see Ingredients)

1 bay leaf

1 sprig thyme

½ cup (90 g) cracked freekeh
(see Ingredients), rinsed

4 spring onions, finely sliced

4 large tomatoes, diced

2 lebanese (small) cucumbers,
halved lengthways and chopped

handful of mint leaves, torn

handful of flat-leaf parsley
leaves, sliced

handful of coriander leaves, sliced

juice of 1 lemon

⅓ cup (80 ml) extra virgin olive oil

salt flakes and cracked
black pepper

Tabbouleh is nice so long as it hasn't been sitting around for ages. Bruised herbs and soggy tomato are clear signs it's not the freshest. Here is a version with structure and flavour. This recipe celebrates spring tomatoes, which lack the sweetness that only summer can bring, and parsley, which is at its very best at this time of year.

I cannot emphasise how important a sharp knife is for this dish. In my opinion, the problem with commercial tabbouleh is that it's whizzed up in a machine, which just bruises everything. A clean, sharp cut on a tomato will not damage the cells surrounding the incision. Sure, juice will seep out on the chopping board, but it shouldn't behave like a running hose and weep forever. As for the herbs, I am actually so pedantic that I bunch them up and slice rather than chop. The blunt force of a straight downwards motion crushes the delicate leaves and in particular blackens the mint. Follow these suggestions and I swear you'll taste the difference.

1 Place the lentils in a saucepan with 2 cups (500 ml) of cold water and add the bay leaf and thyme. Bring to a gentle simmer and cook for 30–40 minutes or until the lentils are tender. Drain and leave to cool.

2 Meanwhile, place the freekeh and 1 cup (250 ml) of water in a small saucepan over medium heat and bring to the boil. Reduce the heat to low, then cover and simmer for 10–15 minutes or until the freekeh is al dente and the water has been absorbed. Remove from the heat and leave to cool.

3 Combine the cooled lentils and freekeh in a bowl, then transfer to serving plates. Top with spring onion, tomato, cucumber, mint, parsley, coriander, lemon juice and olive oil. Season with salt and pepper, and serve immediately. ◗

Sprouted hummus <u>WITH</u> wholemeal flatbreads

Sprouted hummus

½ cup (100 g) dried kabuli chickpeas (see Ingredients)

1 clove garlic, chopped

1½ tablespoons lemon juice

2½ tablespoons unhulled tahini

2 teaspoons salt flakes

½ teaspoon cracked black pepper

½ cup (125 ml) extra virgin olive oil, plus extra for drizzling

½ teaspoon smoked paprika

Wholemeal flatbreads

3 cups (480 g) wholemeal flour

1 cup (250 ml) ice-cold water

¼ cup (60 ml) extra virgin olive oil, plus extra for oiling

2 teaspoons salt flakes

2 teaspoons baking powder

I like to see a few things in the kitchen that need taking care of: a sourdough starter that demands a daily feed; a herb garden out the back door that requires a bit of water and some weeding; a cultured yoghurt that needs a peek to check its progress. It makes the room seem somehow more alive and the food more loved, and I reckon this always shows on the final plates in a good kitchen. (We chefs often aren't very good at looking after our apprentices, our kitchen finances or our personal lives but, hey, that's a whole other book waiting to be written!)

One thing I do like to take care of – and you don't need to run a big fancy kitchen to do it – is sprouts. They only take a few days, maybe a week in the cooler months, and all they need is a daily rinse in cold water and good airflow and light. Get yourself a sprouting bag or jar or just do them in clean muslin cloth. It really doesn't matter what you use: if you keep everything spotless and stay attentive little tails will be sticking out of the seeds in a matter of days – and they taste way better than bought ones. Strictly speaking, there's no sprouting involved in this dish – we're just activating the seed with moisture and warmth – but the chickpeas will still taste so much fresher and grassier.

The breads are a cinch. At a glance it doesn't seem to make sense that a recipe for a typically unleavened style of bread i.e. flatbread contains a raising agent. However, the baking powder is in there to lighten up the wholemeal flour. The resulting breads may be flat, but they are also nice and airy.

1 To sprout the chickpeas for the hummus, chuck them and 2 cups (500 ml) of room-temp water in a bowl. Leave for 24 hours in a shady place, then drain and rinse a few times; they will have tripled in volume. Place the chickpeas in a sprouting bag and hang in your kitchen. Once a day, submerge the bag in plenty of cold water and leave for 30 minutes or so. The water may get a little manky and that's okay, but if it's looking really dirty, rinse the sprouting bag and chickpeas by running cold water through for a minute or so while massaging the sprouts. It is also important to massage the bag gently to unclump the sprouts when soaking each day (especially in the corners where the sprouts can become all bunched up). Rehang the bag. Repeat for 3–4 days, then transfer to an airtight container and keep in the fridge for up to 2 weeks (or you can just throw the sprout bag in the fridge if you don't need to use it). After sprouting it is a good idea to turn the bag inside-out and boil it in water for a minute or two to kill off any nasties, then hang it on the clothesline to get sunny and well aired.

Sprouted hummus WITH wholemeal flatbreads (cont.)

2 For the hummus, place the sprouted chickpeas and garlic in a food processor and blitz to a rough puree. Add the lemon juice, tahini, salt, pepper and 2 tablespoons of warm water and pulse until smooth and well combined. Finish by streaming in the olive oil, pulsing until combined. Just before serving, sprinkle the hummus with paprika and a little more olive oil.

3 For the flatbreads, combine all the ingredients together in a bowl and mix until a dough forms. Turn the dough out onto a lightly floured surface and knead for 1 minute or until smooth. Cover with plastic film and leave to rest for 30 minutes.

4 Divide the dough into six and stretch by hand or roll into 20 cm rounds. Prick the surface with a fork to help prevent air bubbles and lightly oil both sides.

5 Heat an upside-down wok over medium–high heat. Working one at a time, chuck a dough round over the wok and cook for about 1–2 minutes or until a little blistered, then turn over and gently press the dough with a bunched-up tea towel to help the inside cook through. The dough will puff up a little as the steam escapes and will be ready in a minute or so. Serve the flatbreads with the sprouted hummus. ●

Bower spinach, native mint AND desert lime rice paper rolls

80 g rice vermicelli noodles

1 cup (50 g) bower spinach
(or baby spinach)

½ cup (40 g) samphire

1 carrot, peeled and
cut into matchsticks

1 lebanese (small) cucumber,
halved, seeded and
cut into matchsticks

¼ iceberg lettuce, shredded

large handful of basil leaves

large handful of coriander leaves

handful of native mint leaves

1 cup (80 g) bean sprouts

10 desert limes, halved
(or grated zest and cubed
flesh of 1 small lime)

½ cup (70 g) roasted salted
peanuts, roughly chopped

24 × 22 cm rice paper rounds

Dipping sauce

½ cup (125 ml) coconut water

¼ cup (60 ml) light soy sauce

¼ cup (55 g) white sugar

2 tablespoons lime juice

2 tablespoons rice vinegar
or coconut vinegar (see page 55)

2 finger limes, halved and pearls
extracted (or 1 lime, peeled
and cut into 5 mm dice)

2 cloves garlic, crushed

3 small red chillies, finely chopped
(and seeded if you are a chilli fairy)

Finally, native Australian foods are making a resurgence via restaurants and grocers who have the bravery to get with the program. A big nod to the pioneers of the '80s, notably Vic Cherikoff and Andrew Fielke, for bringing these flavours to restaurants thirty years ago, and in turn influencing the recent generation of chefs, and especially to Mike and Gayle Quarmby from The Outback Pride Project. The small explosion in retail availability of native foods is in no small part down to their beliefs, skills and hard work (bloody-minded tenacity is probably a better description). Go to outbackpride.com.au to find out where you can buy these magic ingredients.

Yes, I've said it before and I'll say it again: native foods are the future. We live on possibly one of the oldest land masses in the world and are privileged to walk among the longest continuously surviving culture on earth. That alone is awe-inspiring, but to be able to access some truly 'old' foods not yet selectively bred or tampered with is magnificent for a cook. Native plants are water-wise and perfectly adapted to our climate(s), so they grow abundantly. They are uniquely Australian: sometimes subtle, sometimes bold, often robust in texture, and inspiring to blend and to use. Food has the potential to heal and form trusting relationships between people. Maybe, just maybe, this is a way we can acknowledge, respect and take on some of the wisdom and ways of the people who walked this land some 40 000 years before us.

1 For the dipping sauce, place all the ingredients in a bowl and stir until well combined. Set aside in the fridge.

2 Bring a saucepan of water to the boil and cook the noodles according to the packet instructions. Drain and rinse under cold water.

3 Place the spinach, samphire, carrot, cucumber, lettuce, herbs, bean sprouts and lime in a large bowl and toss to combine. Place the peanuts in a separate bowl.

4 Soak a rice paper round in a bowl of lukewarm water for 15 seconds or until softened, then place on a tea towel. Arrange some of the filling along the middle of the round and sprinkle with peanuts. Fold in the ends and roll up tightly to enclose. Repeat with the remaining rounds, filling and peanuts.

5 Serve the rice paper rolls with the dipping sauce. ◑

400 g palm hearts

½ cup (75 g) plain flour

1 tablespoon salt flakes

½ teaspoon cracked white pepper

1 large free-range egg,
lightly beaten

1 cup (70 g) panko breadcrumbs

1 cup (250 ml) flavour-neutral oil
(such as canola, grapeseed,
rice bran or soybean)

8 slices really 'bad' soft
white bread

¼ small iceberg lettuce, shredded

¼ bunch perilla or basil,
leaves shredded

Sweet Japanese mayo

⅓ cup (80 ml) mirin

2 tablespoons rice vinegar

big pinch of ground wakame or nori
(see Ingredients)

1 teaspoon salt flakes

1 teaspoon dijon mustard

2 free-range egg yolks

1 cup (250 ml) grapeseed
or rice bran oil

Panko-coated palm heart sandwich

Palm hearts and sandwiches are both going to raise a few eyebrows, I know. However, a good sandwich is a good thing indeed. Legend has it the 4th Earl of Sandwich was so busy at the card table he couldn't spare two hands to eat, so he ordered meat tucked between slices of bread. Unfortunately, the sandwich has since been sullied by bad examples and these days is not always a food befitting a Lord.

The Australian palm heart industry is welcome news. With imported tinned palm hearts, it's quite likely the whole palm has been destroyed. Palm Hearts Australia, however, have developed a method that yields the heart without destroying the palm. Palm hearts used to be the principal ingredient in something called Millionaire's salad, in which they were shaved and eaten raw, but here I simmer them to the texture of a cooked waxy spud. Inspired by the Japanese dish *katsu-sando*, I then coat them with breadcrumbs and pop them in a sandwich; the original is essentially a crumbed pork fillet in white bread, so the inclusion of really 'bad' soft white bread in the ingredients is a little nod to this. It also shows my food philosophy is riddled with inconsistencies.

I encourage you to make your own panko as the bought stuff is usually coated in palm oil, an environmental and health travesty. Simply buy a white loaf, remove the crusts and leave it out for a day or so to dry. Run it through the shredding disc of your food processor to make coarse crumbs, then spread them over a baking tray and toast in a 140°C fan-forced (160°C conventional) oven for 5–8 minutes until dry but not coloured. Easy. Bought Japanese-style mayo also often contains high fructose corn syrup and MSG, and it remains one of my proudest kitchen moments to synthesise a food full of nasties using nice stuff.

Yes, there is a bit of mucking around to make this but I reckon the result is a sandwich befitting a lord and a millionaire, and that was the aim. Of course, they do say we eat with our eyes, so if you can't be bothered you could just look at the photo while eating a triangle sandwich from the service station – although I don't imagine it will be quite the same . . .

1 To prepare the palm hearts, use a small sharp knife to remove the outer layers, exposing the tender core. Place in a large saucepan of salted cold water and bring to the boil, then reduce the heat and simmer for 1 hour. Drain, then cut the palm hearts into fingers, about 8 cm long, 3 cm wide and 1 cm thick.

Panko-coated palm heart sandwich <u>(cont.)</u>

2 To make the sweet Japanese mayo, place the mirin in a very small saucepan over low heat and simmer for a minute until reduced by half. Remove from the heat and add the rice vinegar, wakame or nori, salt and mustard. Transfer to a bowl, then add the egg yolks and whisk to combine. Slowly drizzle in the oil while whisking. Place the mayo in the fridge until ready to serve; leftovers will keep for up to a week.

3 Place the flour, salt and pepper in a small bowl. Place the egg in a separate bowl and the panko breadcrumbs on a plate. Dust the palm heart fingers in the seasoned flour, shaking off any excess, then dredge them through the egg, again shaking off excess, before rolling them in the breadcrumbs.

4 Place a frying pan over medium heat and add 1 cm of oil for shallow-frying. Add the panko-coated palm hearts and cook for 1 minute on each side until golden and crispy. Using a spider or slotted spoon, remove them from the pan and drain on paper towel.

5 Spread way too much mayonnaise over the bread slices. Top half of them with lettuce and perilla, then the palm heart fingers. Top with bread and cut each sandwich into three. ◑

Tofu larp

3 tablespoons jasmine rice

200 g firm tofu, frozen and thawed
(see Ingredients), then crumbled
into 5 mm pieces

pinch of white sugar

1 teaspoon salt flakes,
plus extra if needed

1 fat lemongrass stalk,
white part finely chopped

3 red shallots, thinly sliced

1 small clove garlic, finely chopped

1 bird's eye chilli, chopped

1 tablespoon Thai-seasoned
soy sauce

¼ cup (60 ml) lime juice

small handful of coriander leaves

small handful of mint leaves, torn

1 tablespoon shredded
sawtooth coriander

½ teaspoon cracked white pepper

20 betel leaves

Tofu that is frozen, thawed and crumbled takes on a mince-like texture that is perfect for this Thai salad. It soaks up all the delicious flavours and the result is anything but bland. In fact, after giving this recipe a whirl, you may wonder why anyone uses chicken instead. The ground toasted rice gently pulls the mixture together and adds a wonderful toasty note. I use Thai-seasoned soy sauce in many of my recipes because it has a few more flavour notes than straight light soy and it helps fill the gap left by omitting fish sauce from vego dishes. It's not essential though and you can always use any light soy if you don't have it.

The sawtooth coriander is another bonus. It's a funny little plant with serrated-edged leaves close to the soil, and a bunch of big seedpods and really spiky leaves nearer the top. These top clusters of leaves are far too prickly to eat, but the leaves at the base contain all the coriander flavour with a far more robust structure than the soft-leaf variety. There's nothing wussy or delicate about it: this is coriander that has been working out in the gym. If you can't get it, just use regular coriander, but have a think about popping some in your vegie patch: it survives without love, and you'll have a decent supply throughout the colder months and into late spring.

1 Toast the rice in a small heavy-based frying pan over medium heat, shaking the pan until the rice is slightly fawn in colour. Remove from the heat and leave to cool slightly, then pound or use a spice grinder to grind to the consistency of coarse cracked pepper.

2 Place the crumbled tofu in the centre of a tea towel. Bring the corners together and twist gently to extract the moisture; be firm but gentle – you want to extract as much liquid as possible without crushing the tofu.

3 Heat ¼ cup (60 ml) of water in a frying pan over medium heat. Add the sugar and salt, then the lemongrass, shallot, garlic and half the chilli, and simmer for 1 minute until a little soft. Add the soy sauce and crumbled tofu and simmer, stirring, for another minute. Remove from the heat and fold in 1 tablespoon of toasted rice, then turn the heat down and continue to cook, stirring, for about 30 seconds until the rice absorbs most of the remaining liquid.

4 Remove the pan from the heat and add the lime juice, half the herbs and the pepper. Check the seasoning – you want the salad to have a good balance of hot, sour and salty, so adjust accordingly.

5 To serve, place a heaped teaspoon of larp on each betel leaf and garnish with the remaining toasted rice, chilli and herbs. ◗

Serves 4

Pie floater

200 g all-butter puff pastry,
thawed if frozen, brought to
room temperature

200 g Mushroom paste
(see Basics)

1 cup (250 ml) pouring cream

½ cup (125 ml) milk

3 free-range eggs

small handful of flat-leaf parsley
leaves, chopped

2 teaspoons salt flakes

cracked black pepper

Tomato chutney

2½ tablespoons flavour-neutral oil
(see page 33)

2 cloves garlic, crushed

2 tablespoons chopped ginger

1 onion, chopped

400 g tomatoes, peeled, cored
and roughly chopped

2 strips orange peel, pith removed

1 clove

70 ml white wine vinegar

40 g brown sugar

salt flakes and cracked
black pepper

Pea soup

100 g butter

2 golden shallots, finely diced

1 clove garlic, crushed

400 g peas (1–1.2 kg in pods)

salt flakes and cracked
white pepper

2 tablespoons white vinegar

Fast food isn't always bad food. Way before the multinational fast-food chains arrived, we had the pie cart. Adelaide embraced the traditional Yorkshire combo of pie and peas more enthusiastically than anywhere else in Australia. By the late 1800s, there were thirteen pie carts lining the streets in an L-shape near the railway station. Grainy post-WW1 photos show a small army of predominantly young males there, freshly turfed out of the pubs – this was the era of the 'six o'clock swill' and the pie carts benefited from the early closing, selling the perfect combination of stodge to fill pickled punters' bellies. (Now I really must be getting old, because the early closing of pubs seems to me like a great way of ensuring a family ate dinner together.)

Since its last pie cart closed in 2007, Adelaide's just not the same. I had my last pie floater that year and decided to put a fancy one on my menu in honour of the tradition. I opted for fresh green peas and a lush creamy mushroom paste instead of the usual meaty filling, but it nonetheless became a hit and didn't leave the menu until I left the restaurant. The best bit? A smidge of vinegar (traditionally malt) rained into the pea soup just before eating. It's a last-minute job as it discolours the vibrant green soup, but it really makes the peas come alive.

And if you want to relive another era sadly passed, crack a ginger beer too. At one pie cart in Adelaide, they served it directly from the keg. The mention of this brings happy tears to the eyes of more than a few old boys around my hometown. To see the weariness of a life well lived momentarily lift as they perk up is one of those little bits of magic that has me smiling for the rest of the day.

1 For the tomato chutney, heat the oil in a heavy-based saute or frying pan over medium–low heat. Add the garlic, ginger and onion and fry for 5 minutes, stirring occasionally, then add the tomato, orange peel, clove, vinegar and sugar. Cover the pan, reduce the heat to low and simmer gently for 40 minutes until the chutney is rich and chunky, stirring regularly to prevent burning. Season with salt and pepper, and set aside. (Leftover chutney will keep in a sterilised jar in the fridge for up to a month.)

2 For the pea soup, heat the butter in a large heavy-based saucepan over medium–low heat. Add the shallot and garlic, then cover with a lid and cook for 5 minutes or until the shallot is soft. Add the peas and saute briefly, then add 2 cups (500 ml) of water and bring to the boil. Immediately remove from the heat and use a stick blender to puree until smooth; if the soup is too thick, add a little more water. Season with salt and pepper, and immediately place in the fridge to chill.

Pie floater (cont.)

3 Preheat the oven to 180°C fan-forced (200°C conventional).

4 Roll the puff pastry to a thickness of 2.5 mm and cut out four 15 cm squares. Line four deep pie tins (about 200 ml capacity) with the pastry, leaving it overhanging, then line the pastry with baking paper and fill with baking beans or rice. Chill in the fridge for 10 minutes.

5 Place the pie tins on a baking tray and blind-bake the pastry for 15 minutes or until just set and beginning to colour in places. Remove the baking beans and paper, and set the pastry aside. Turn down the oven temperature to 170°C fan-forced (190°C conventional).

6 While the pastry is blind-baking, combine the mushroom paste and cream in a small saucepan over medium heat and simmer for about 5 minutes until reduced by a third. Add the milk, then immediately remove the pan from the heat. Transfer the mixture to a bowl and pop it in the fridge for 10–15 minutes.

7 Whisk the eggs in a bowl. Pour the cooled cream and mushroom mixture over the top, whisking to combine. Add the parsley, salt and pepper.

8 Pour the mixture into the pastry shells, then return them to the oven and bake for 10 minutes or until the filling is just set. Be careful – overcooking will cause the filling to become rubbery, so it's better to take the pies out of the oven while the filling still wobbles ever so slightly.

9 To serve, gently reheat the pea soup and pour into shallow bowls. Place a pie in the centre and top with a dollop of tomato chutney. Splash the vinegar over the pea soup at the last minute. ◐

Serves 4

Ma po tofu

1 cup (30 g) dried
shiitake mushrooms

100 g firm tofu, frozen and thawed
(see Ingredients)

2½ tablespoons Chinese hot chilli
paste (or Korean hot pepper paste)

¼ cup (60 ml) shaohsing

¼ cup (60 ml) light soy sauce

1 teaspoon sesame oil

1 teaspoon white sugar

1 teaspoon ground sichuan pepper

100 ml peanut oil

1½ tablespoons fermented
black beans, roughly chopped
(or black bean sauce)

3 cloves garlic, crushed

1 tablespoon grated ginger

3 spring onions, finely sliced

1 tablespoon cornflour mixed
with 2 tablespoons water

400 g silken firm tofu, cut
into 8 cm × 4 cm pieces

steamed jasmine rice, to serve

This may seem like a winter dish but as the weather warms I like my food to heat up as well. This one certainly isn't shy: together the sichuan peppercorns, ginger and hot chilli paste deliver a multi-dimensional heat that will have you sweating a little. Don't be put off by your first taste when the dish is still on the stove; eating this with steamed jasmine rice moderates the pleasant pain.

The frozen and thawed tofu (also used in the Tofu larp recipe on page 36) brings a mincemeat-like element to the sauce but the real punch comes from ground-up shiitakes, the kings of mushroom texture. As with all recipes heavily laden with mushrooms, you need to slightly over-season with salt. Here this is achieved by adding black beans and a copious amount of light soy, which is to Chinese cookery as salt is to French cookery.

Don't get bogged down by the chilli paste. It's basically a fiery concoction of pureed chilli with some sort of acidity to help etch that heat onto your palate. Just about every Asian culture has a version and as long as the paste is thick and potent it will do the trick here.

1 Soak the shiitakes in 2 cups (500 ml) of warm water for 15–20 minutes. Remove the shiitakes, squeezing out any excess water into the bowl, then cut off and discard the stems. Strain the soaking water and set it aside. Put the shiitakes in a food processor and pulse to the texture of minced meat. Set aside.

2 Squeeze the excess liquid out of the thawed, frozen tofu, then rub it between your hands to crumble to the same consistency as the shiitakes. Set aside.

3 Combine the shiitake soaking water with the chilli paste, shaohsing, soy sauce, sesame oil, sugar and half of the sichuan pepper. Set the sauce aside.

4 Heat the peanut oil in a wok over medium heat, then add the minced shiitakes and black beans and fry until well coloured, about 5 minutes. Add the crumbled tofu and continue to fry for a minute or two. Add the garlic, ginger and spring onion whites and cook, stirring, for about 2 minutes until fragrant. Pour in the sauce and bring up to a gentle simmer for 3–5 minutes. Stream in the cornflour mixture while stirring, then simmer for another minute or two until the sauce has thickened to a creamy, rich consistency.

5 Divide the silken firm tofu among serving bowls and pour the sauce over the top. Leave for a minute to warm the tofu, then garnish with the spring onion greens and remaining sichuan pepper. Serve with steamed jasmine rice.

Smoked tofu kedgeree

2 cups (400 g) long-grain
brown rice (or basmati rice)

salt flakes and cracked
black pepper

4 free-range eggs

100 ml ghee

1 onion, diced

½ teaspoon finely chopped ginger

2 cloves garlic, crushed

2 tablespoons madras curry powder

100 g natural yoghurt

juice of 1 lemon

100 g smoked tofu, ripped

handful of flat-leaf parsley
leaves, chopped

handful of coriander leaves

Ever since we harnessed flame and started chucking things on or in it, the smell of food charring, being caressed by smoke, or spitting out and landing on hot coals has signalled 'dinnertime'. But it doesn't have to be meat that is smokin'. Tofu is brilliant at sucking up flavours and aromas, and smoke is no exception. You can either buy smoked tofu or smoke your own (see Ingredients for more).

Traditionally a British Indian breakfast dish, kedgeree also makes a great lunch or light supper. You can use some leftover rice to knock it up but it's a quick and easy dish from scratch. The most time-consuming part is peeling the eggs. Generally, old eggs are easier to peel as the air pocket between the white and the shell is larger. This is why old eggs float (or at least sit upright) in water and hard-boil well from a cold start, which also helps prevent the shells cracking. If your eggs are fresh, I suggest you do a 'hot start' and shock the whites into setting quickly, then refresh them in iced water for an hour or so, otherwise they may be hard to peel.

Don't worry if you don't have madras curry powder. It's fine to use whatever blend you have on hand. The madras is heavy on turmeric and adds a nice breezy colour to the rice, which I like but it is not essential.

1 Place the rice in a large heavy-based saucepan and cover with 3 cups (750 ml) of cold water and a good pinch of salt. Bring to a simmer over medium heat, then reduce the heat to very low and cover with a tight-fitting lid. Cook for about 18 minutes or until the rice is tender. Remove from the heat and fluff up the rice with a fork. Set aside.

2 While the rice is cooking, place the eggs in a small saucepan and cover with cold water by about 1 cm. Place over medium–low heat and bring to a gentle simmer. Cook for 4 minutes, then refresh the eggs under cold water to stop them cooking further. When cool enough to handle, peel and quarter the eggs, then cover them and set aside at room temperature.

3 Place a heavy-based saute or frying pan over medium heat. Add the ghee, onion, ginger and garlic and stir to combine, then cover with a lid and cook for 5 minutes or until the onion is translucent and soft. Add the curry powder and saute for 2 minutes, then add the cooked rice and the yoghurt, stirring until the rice is well coated. Add the lemon juice and season well with salt and pepper, tossing to combine.

4 Divide the rice among plates. Arrange the egg quarters, smoked tofu and herbs on top and serve. ●

Serves 2

40 g gruyere, sliced

4 thick slices bread

½ cup (125 g) purple sauerkraut

Fries

4 starchy potatoes (such as colibans, kennebecs or russets), cut into thick chips

salt flakes

flavour-neutral oil (see page 33), for deep-frying

Lentil patties

½ cup (100 g) unhulled red lentils (see Ingredients)

30 g butter

1 large golden shallot, finely sliced

20 g plain flour

1 teaspoon dijon mustard

1 teaspoon green peppercorns, crushed

2 tablespoons extra virgin olive oil

Russian mayo

1 free-range egg

1 teaspoon dijon mustard

½ teaspoon salt flakes

2 tablespoons lemon juice or white vinegar

200 ml extra virgin olive oil

2 tablespoons chopped chives

pinch of smoked paprika

¼ cup (60 ml) passata or tomato ketchup

1 tablespoon boiling water

I hate vegie burgers, <u>so</u> the vegie reuben

I've put it out there that I don't like vegie burgers, but I'll make an exception for the crazy crew from Veggie Velo who, led by the dreadlocked all-round nice guy Manu, pedal-power their way around the Adelaide CBD making awesome specimens. I can't make them that good, however, so I'll stick to an approximation of that New York classic, the Reuben. The exact ingredients are hotly debated, but what's not to love about tomato, mayo and gooey cheese?

For this vegie version, we make a slab of mushed-up lentils seasoned with green peppercorns and mustard, then give it a quick set and a fry to exploit the lentils' sweetness. It brings a great textural surprise to the sandwich and served with real thrice-fried fries this becomes a substantial meal.

1 For the fries, place the potato in a large saucepan and cover with cold water and a pinch of salt. Bring to the boil over high heat, then reduce the heat and simmer gently over medium–low for 10–12 minutes or until really soft. (Don't allow the water to boil rapidly or the potato will fall apart; you want the chips to remain intact.) Drain on paper towel, then spread out on a tray and leave in the fridge for 1 hour. (This will help to set the potato in preparation for frying.)

2 Meanwhile, for the lentil patties, place the lentils and 2 cups (500 ml) of water in a small saucepan. Bring to a simmer over medium heat and cook gently for 45 minutes or until the lentils are mushy and there is very little or no water left.

3 While the lentils are cooking, make the Russian mayo. Place the egg in a bowl and whisk in the mustard, salt and lemon juice or vinegar. Very slowly drizzle in the olive oil, whisking continuously. Fold through the chives, paprika, passata or ketchup and boiling water. Place in the fridge until ready to serve.

4 When the lentils are ready, line a baking tray with baking paper. Place a heavy-based saucepan over medium heat and add the butter. Fry the shallot for a minute or so until just soft, then add the flour and cook, stirring, for a minute until the ingredients bind together. Stir in the lentils, mustard and peppercorns and cook for another minute. Turn the lentil mixture out onto the prepared tray and cover with baking paper. Use a palette knife to smooth and compress the lentils into a patty, then pop it in the fridge for 1 hour to set.

I hate vegie burgers, so the vegie reuben
(cont.)

5 Pour the oil for the fries into a large heavy-based saucepan or deep-fryer until two-thirds full. Add the chilled potato chips and bring the oil to 100°C over medium–low heat – you will notice the oil gently bubbling as the water in the potato evaporates. Once this temperature is reached, fry the chips for 10 minutes until the skin is really crisp but not coloured. Remove with a spider or slotted spoon, drain on paper towel and return the fries to the fridge for 30 minutes.

6 Reheat the frying oil to 180°C and add the chilled fries. Cook for 5 minutes until crisp and golden. Drain on paper towel and season with salt.

7 Preheat the grill to high. Place the gruyere over two slices of bread. Grill all the sliced bread for 4 minutes or until the gruyere is melted and browned, leaving the other side untoasted.

8 Cut into the lentil patty into two. Place a heavy-based frying pan over medium heat and add the olive oil. Fry the patties for about a minute on each side, until well coloured.

9 Place a pattie on each slice of plain toasted bread, then add the sauerkraut and a tablespoon of the mayo. Top with the remaining toast, cheese-side down. ◗

Rice noodles WITH tofu, chives AND peanuts

400 g firm tofu

½ cup (70 g) unsalted peanuts

1½ cups (375 ml) flavour-neutral oil (see page 33)

¼ cup (60 ml) tamarind concentrate or rice vinegar

2 tablespoons coconut palm sugar (see page 70)

2 free-range eggs

2 red shallots, sliced

⅛ teaspoon white peppercorns, pounded

⅛ teaspoon dried chilli flakes (the one with seeds and all)

3 cloves garlic, crushed

50 g salted preserved turnip slivers, salt rubbed off, diced

100 g dried medium (5 mm–1 cm) flat rice noodles, soaked in warm water for 10 minutes, then drained

⅓ cup (80 ml) really good tomato ketchup

¼ cup (60 ml) Thai-seasoned soy sauce (see page 36)

1 bunch garlic chives, chopped into 2.5 cm lengths

200 g bean sprouts

juice of 1 lime

For all intents and purposes, this is a vegie pad Thai. However, since the formation of the Thai Delicious Committee, I wouldn't dare call it that. Somewhat like the French Appellation d'Origine Contrôlée, this Thai government body aims to keep its national culinary icons authentic, and I'll respect that. They even trialled a robotic tasting device to audit dishes, involving a bunch of wires and hooha with electronic circuitry connected to a computer, so they are definitely serious (albeit a little wacky). It's an age-old food debate. In the red corner, you have the chefs who believe in mad technology, new chemical isolates and breaking ground with method. In the blue corner, the traditionalists who will go to every possible length to research the origins and traditions of a dish and try and recreate the *methode*. Me, I'm in the magenta corner! I like to adapt a dish with ingredients available at my end of the world, and in this case for people who don't eat fish, while at the same time trying to honour the basic cornerstones. Some would say the ketchup is an aberration, but I always add it. Anyway. The turnip and soy combine here with tomato and tamarind to produce the correct balance of flavours, and it's delicious. The most enjoyable part? Fistfuls of sprouts and chives with a bit of bite. The preserved turnip is easy to find: just follow your nose to the ominous and aromatic corner of the Asian grocers and the mad array of vegetarian 'offal'.

1 Wrap the tofu in a tea towel and place on a draining board. Press with a 1 kg weight for an hour to remove excess moisture, then cut into 1 cm cubes.

2 Place the peanuts in a saucepan of cold water over medium heat. Bring to the boil, then reduce the heat and simmer for 10 minutes. Drain the peanuts in a strainer. Heat the oil in a small saucepan over medium heat, add the drained peanuts and bring to a simmer – they will bubble for about 10 minutes as the water evaporates. As soon as the pan begins to go quiet and a roasted peanut smell develops, remove the peanuts with a slotted spoon, then drain on paper towel. Reserve 100 ml of the frying oil. Roughly crush the nuts, then set aside.

3 Combine the tamarind or vinegar and palm sugar in a small bowl and stir until the sugar dissolves. Set aside.

4 Preheat a wok over high heat and add the reserved frying oil. When almost smoking, add the tofu and stir-fry for a minute or so until crisp and golden, then move it to the side of the wok. Crack the eggs into a bowl and slide into the wok, then pop the yolks and leave for a minute or two until almost set. Push the eggs to the side with the tofu. Add the shallot, pepper, chilli, garlic and turnip to the wok and stir-fry for a minute or so until aromatic. Add the noodles and fry for 2 minutes. Add the tamarind or vinegar mixture, tomato ketchup, soy sauce, garlic chives and bean sprouts, tossing to combine. Squeeze the lime juice over the top and throw in the peanuts. Serve. ◖

Cashew, green mango AND spinach egg nets

4 free-range eggs

salt flakes

½ bunch coriander, roots rinsed,
leaves chopped

4 cloves garlic, chopped

10 white peppercorns

2 tablespoons flavour-neutral
oil (see page 33), plus 2 cups
(500 ml) for deep-frying

1 cup (150 g) roasted cashews,
roughly chopped

60 g baby spinach, shredded

2 tablespoons Thai-seasoned
soy sauce (see page 36)

1 tablespoon coconut palm sugar
(see page 70)

½ lemongrass stalk, finely sliced

2 red shallots, sliced

2 bird's eye chillies, finely sliced

¼ cup (30 g) grated green mango

Just because a mango is green doesn't mean it's a green mango! Green in this case generally refers to the varieties that are palatable when mature yet remain green fleshed. We are lucky in Australia as many green varieties grow well in the northern states and are in abundance in late spring through summer. There are exceptions to the above rule: one variety that eats well green, but will still ripen to a sweet juicy orange-fleshed fruit, is the nam doc mai. Many people would consider this addition 'inauthentic' as they are not generally prized as a green mango in Asia, but when the outer skin is white to green in colour it is great in this salad and provides crunchy, slightly sour notes. A green papaya in place of mango will do the trick as well.

Making the egg nets is a lot of fun. It involves dripping the egg mix over the hot oil to create a spider's web. There's no particular need for precision: after a few passes over the wok the strands of egg will bind together forming a 15 cm or so web. A little trial and error with the speed your hand travels and the amount of dripping egg and you'll have it nailed in no time.

1 Lightly whisk the eggs with 2 teaspoons of salt – do not overbeat. Strain through a fine strainer into a bowl, then cover with plastic film and place in the fridge to chill overnight.

2 Using a mortar and pestle, pound the coriander roots, garlic, peppercorns and a pinch of salt to a smooth paste. Heat 2 tablespoons of oil in a frying pan, add the paste and fry until fragrant and golden. Add the cashews, spinach, soy sauce and palm sugar and stir for a few seconds until the spinach has wilted. Set aside to cool.

3 Bring the chilled egg up to room temperature. Pour 2 cups (500 ml) of oil into a small wok and place over medium heat until just shimmering. Dip your hand in the egg and slowly move it in a crisscross action 3 cm above the wok, allowing the egg to fall into the hot oil, then circle the outside to form a net. Make sure you do not move too quickly as the strands will become too fine and break. The nets will set in about 20 seconds and do not require turning – just use a spider or spatula to carefully remove them from the oil. Drain on paper towel. Repeat with the remaining egg to make 12–16 nets.

4 Add the lemongrass, shallot, chilli, green mango and coriander leaves to the cooled cashew mixture and stir until well combined.

5 Lay out an egg net and spread 2 tablespoons of cashew mixture over the bottom third. Roll up to enclose. Repeat with the remaining egg nets and cashew mixture. Serve immediately. ●

Stir-fried cucumber <u>WITH</u> pickled bean sprouts

1 large cucumber, halved lengthways and cut into 1 cm thick slices

⅓ cup (80 ml) flavour-neutral oil (see page 33)

2.5 cm ginger, peeled and cut into matchsticks

4 cloves garlic, finely chopped

½ teaspoon white sugar

4 spring onions, green parts cut into 5 cm batons, white parts finely chopped

10 g dried black fungus, soaked in hot water for 15 minutes, then chopped

1 × 300 g tin water chestnuts, drained and halved on an angle

80 g roasted cashews

2 tablespoons light soy sauce

¼ cup (60 ml) shaohsing

½ teaspoon sesame oil

Pickled bean sprouts (see Basics), to serve

steamed jasmine rice, to serve

It might sound stupid to freeze a cucumber and then cook it, but hang in there with me. This process allows you to caramelise the outside of the fruit in the wok without turning the flesh to mush, delivering a whole new flavour. 'Fruit?' I hear you say. Yes, like tomato, chilli, eggplant and pumpkin, botanically speaking cucumber is a fruit, even though in culinary terms it is referred to as a vegetable. I'm only pointing this out in the hope you will think I am so clever, you'll trust me enough to give the recipe a pop and stir-fry a cucumber.

Then, just as I convince you to give this a try, I go and put you off again by including black fungus in the recipe – but hang in there! The resulting stir-fry is an amazing balance of textures: the juicy, firm cucumber, the crunchy roasted cashews and the rubbery fungus. If you can get past the name and give it a go, you won't regret it. You'll find it in the dried goods section of Asian grocers and you can even buy it in pre-cut strips in some places.

The pickled bean sprouts are really easy to do and bring another interesting texture to the final meal. Make them while the cucumber is freezing and you're in for a treat.

1 Pop the sliced cucumber in the freezer for an hour or so.

2 When you are ready to make the stir-fry, make sure you have all your ingredients ready to go as this is a fast dish to cook! Preheat a wok over the highest heat for a minute or two, then add the oil and swirl it around. Fry the ginger and garlic until lightly browned, then add the cucumber, sugar, spring onion, black fungus and water chestnuts and cook for a further minute.

3 Add the cashews, soy sauce, shaohsing and sesame oil, and fry for a further minute or until the cucumber is heated through.

4 Serve immediately with pickled bean sprouts and steamed jasmine rice. ◗

Dirty fried eggs <u>WITH</u> green chilli sambal

1 cup (200 g) medium-grain brown rice

2 cups (500 ml) flavour-neutral oil (see page 33)

4 extra-large free-range eggs

¼ teaspoon cracked white pepper

2 tablespoons vegetarian oyster sauce

1 spring onion, sliced

handful of coriander leaves

Crispy shallot chips (see Basics), to garnish

1 tablespoon toasted black sesame seeds

Green chilli sambal

100 g large green chillies, stems removed

½ teaspoon salt flakes

2 tablespoons coconut vinegar or rice vinegar

Eggs. You've boiled them, you've poached them, you've baked them, but have you deep-fried them? If you eat super-clean and steam everything, you may be horrified by this thought, but I assure you that not all deep-fried food is 'dirty'. If your oil is clean and your temperature correct, the eggs in this recipe should retain very little oil once you've slipped them out of the wok and drained them. Chinese chefs crack the eggs straight into shimmering oil but as you are about to witness something akin to the big bang theory occur in your wok (kaboom and rapid expansion), I suggest you crack them into a bowl first and gently slide them into the oil. My forearms are peppered with wok scars and I quite like an opportunity to add to my ink-free tattoo collection but I understand if you don't.

You absolutely don't have to make your own sambal but when chillies are cheap or abundant in your garden it makes sense. I think it gives you a sense of pride and ownership in your cooking that money can't buy and this is what makes some food greater than the mere sum of its parts. It's the difference between making a card and sending an email for someone's birthday. The coconut vinegar adds a light backnote of perfume. You'll find it in Asian grocers and health-food shops.

1 To make the green chilli sambal, place the chillies and salt in a food processor and blend to the texture of coarse breadcrumbs. Place in a bowl, cover with muslin cloth and leave in a really warm place, such as outside in the sun for a couple of days. The chillies will start to smell a little 'funky' and almost fermented, which is fine – just stir them occasionally to remove the top crust. Add the vinegar and transfer to a sterilised jar. The sambal will keep for up to a year in the pantry.

2 Rinse the rice and place it in a saucepan with 1½ cups (375 ml) of water. Bring to a simmer over high heat, then cover with a tight-fitting lid, reduce the heat to low and cook for 18 minutes or until the water has been absorbed. Remove from the heat and leave to stand for 10 minutes before fluffing with a fork to separate the grains. Divide the rice between plates or bowls.

3 Heat the oil in a wok over high heat until shimmering. Crack 2 eggs into a shallow bowl and carefully slip them into the hot oil; be careful as the oil may splash. Cook for 2 minutes or until the eggs puff up and become crisp and golden around the edges. Using a spider or slotted spoon, carefully remove the fried eggs from the oil and place on top of one lot of rice. Repeat with the remaining eggs. Season the fried eggs with pepper and spoon over the oyster sauce. Garnish with spring onion, coriander, shallot chips, green chilli sambal and black sesame seeds. ●

Artichoke stacciare

4 globe artichokes

juice of ½ lemon

salt flakes and cracked
black pepper

½ cup (140 g) Mushroom paste
(see Basics)

2 free-range eggs, lightly beaten

¼ cup (20 g) finely grated
parmesan

1 tablespoon finely chopped
flat-leaf parsley

1½ teaspoons truffle salt

Nothing says spring like flowers and artichoke is the bud of the thistle before it blooms. If you're growing your own, nip 'em off with about 10 cm of stem when they are tightly wound and heavy; loose, open leaves are nature's way of saying the artichoke is past its 'best before'. The choke is the immature flower hiding away in the bud. It seems to be the artichoke's best and worst feature: when you're preparing the artichoke for eating it's a little pesky to dig out, but if you let the petals open, the choke morphs into a stunning purple flower. You won't be ableto eat the artichoke by this stage but the neighbourhood bees will love you for it. They're my favourite flower too and I want them on my coffin when I finally pop my clogs.

Artichokes are really not hard to prepare: you can have them trimmed, de-choked and cooked in the time it takes a takeaway pizza to be delivered (and the tinned ones they chuck on said pizzas don't hold a candle to the real-deal fresh ones). The only drawback is the stubborn black stains on your hands you'll carry around if you don't glove up when preparing them – although you might want to wear these as a badge of honour, showing you did some serious cheffing at home. The soup itself is a rustic mess of dislodged petals, chunks of heart, ripped-up egg threads and diced mushrooms, but the broth is light and refreshing.

1 To prepare the artichokes, cut off the top third of the leaves, trimming the older outer leaves back until you see a very pale green-yellow patch on the base of the leaves. Scoop out the hairy choke from the centre, then nip the stem about 5 cm from the lowest leaves. I sometimes run a peeler down the stems if they look a little woody (as you would with old asparagus). Then just plonk the artichokes into 2 cups (500 ml) of water with a squeeze of lemon juice to prevent them discolouring.

2 Bring a large saucepan of salted water to a simmer over high heat. Add the artichokes and simmer for 30 minutes until the stems are soft and the leaves are tender. (You may need to place a plate on top to sink the chokes and ensure even cooking.) Drain and, when the artichokes are cool enough to handle, cut them into halves or quarters depending on their size.

3 Fill a saucepan with 1 litre of water and a tablespoon of salt and add the mushroom paste. Bring up to a simmer over medium heat, without stirring.

4 Meanwhile, place the beaten eggs and parmesan with half the parsley and 1 teaspoon of truffle salt in a small bowl and season with pepper. Whisk together until well combined.

5 Stream the egg mixture into the hot mushroom broth, whisking continuously. Reduce the heat to low and cook gently for 2 minutes, then add the artichokes and warm through for a minute or so.

6 Sprinkle the remaining parsley and truffle salt over the top and serve. ◑

Serves 4

Green olive AND ricotta dumplings WITH sage

400 g fresh ricotta

1 free-range egg, beaten

2 cups (320 g) baker's flour

1½ teaspoons salt flakes

⅓ cup (25 g) finely grated parmesan, plus extra, shaved, to garnish

½ cup (60 g) pitted green olives, chopped

olive oil, for brushing

80 g butter, roughly chopped

¼ bunch sage, leaves picked

grated zest and juice of ½ lemon

cracked black pepper

Thanks to all the imported expertise we gained through migration, we grow and cure olives exceptionally well in Australia. A green olive is one picked fat but young and not yet ripe, then cured. The firm texture of an olive cured well is essential to this dish: it adds surprise to the otherwise smooth, soft texture of the gnocchi. My favourite olives for this are the Spanish variety manzanilla, because you can shake up a martini while cooking and pop one in, but I also love a good verdale, originating from the South of France and now a common sight in South Australia. They are somewhat unfashionable because the seed-to-flesh ratio renders them less commercially viable than other varieties, but they are magic.

The trick to making the dough is remembering you're trying to create 'earlobe' texture in the final dumpling. This means a little softness and a little resistance. Overwork the dough and the gluten will render the dumplings riot-control bullets. A final and brief trip to a hot pan with nut-brown butter and sage knocks some depth of flavour onto the surface of the dumplings and they become perfectly crispy and golden.

1 Place the ricotta in a fine sieve over a bowl and cover with plastic film. Leave to drain overnight in the fridge.

2 Place the drained ricotta in a large bowl with the egg, flour, salt and grated parmesan. Gently mix by cutting through with your fingertips or a pastry card – do not work it like a bread dough! – then add the olives.

3 Dust the benchtop with flour, then tip out the dough and roll it into a sausage about 30 cm long and 4 cm thick. It is very soft and requires a deft touch, so just knock it to and fro using the heel of your hand. Cut the roll into 1 cm thick discs. Re-dust with flour, then stand the discs upright and lightly press them with a fork to flatten them into dumplings.

4 Brush a baking tray with olive oil. Bring a large saucepan of salted water to the boil, then reduce to a simmer over medium heat. Working in batches, drop the dumplings into the water and cook for 2–3 minutes or until they float to the surface. Using a slotted spoon, carefully remove and drain the dumplings, then pop them on the oiled tray.

5 Heat the butter in a frying pan over medium–high heat until it foams and turns golden brown. Add the sage and lemon zest and fry for about 1 minute or until the sage is crispy, then add the dumplings and fry for 1 minute until coloured up a little.

6 Serve immediately with shaved parmesan, lemon juice and black pepper sprinkled over the top. ●

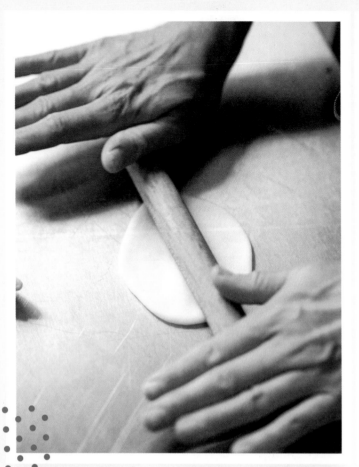

Pea shoot dumplings

2 tablespoons virgin coconut oil

300 g snow pea shoots

¼ bunch garlic chives,
finely chopped

2 tablespoons shaohsing

2 tablespoons light soy sauce

1 teaspoon salt flakes

½ teaspoon cracked white pepper

Dough

¼ cup (60 g) virgin coconut oil

1 cup (250 ml) boiling water

½ teaspoon salt flakes

1½ cups (180 g) wheat starch
or 1½ cups (250 g) cornflour

½ cup (60 g) tapioca starch

Dipping sauce

½ cup (125 ml) Chinese black
vinegar

2 tablespoons light soy sauce

2.5 cm ginger, peeled and grated

1 bird's eye chilli, chopped

¼ teaspoon sesame oil

Dumplings are the culinary equivalent of kittens – cute! You just can't not be happy eating them. Oh, hang on, I didn't mean that quite how it sounded, but I think you get the picture: they are whimsical and fun, and they make everyone smile. The only 'but' is that they need to be plump and full, as though they have little bellies. I reckon thin, pointy dumplings look a bit mean and joyless. Luckily this is easy to achieve as you just overfill them so that they bulge like chubby parcels. The folding technique is one that leaves many people looking like they have two left hands but once mastered you can pop the dumplings out in seconds. To this end, we have included a few pics of the process because we reckon dumpling-making is an important life skill. It's a life that hasn't reached its full potential unless you practise the craft and become your household's own dumpling master . . .

Wheat starch is wheat flour sans the gluten. Grab a packet from the Asian grocer or just use cornflour, which behaves the same. The tapioca starch creates elasticity, which prevents the skin from cracking when you are shaping the dumplings. The Chinese black vinegar in the sauce is rich and complex, a little like balsamic. Snow pea shoots are the ones with immature leaves and small curling tendrils, definitely not those sad sprouts that pubs were so fond of in the '80s. No one ever ate them – and if you did you are probably about to skip this recipe – but I assure you the shoots are a different story: sweet and herbaceous.

1 For the dipping sauce, mix all the ingredients together in a small bowl.

2 For the dough, place the coconut oil, boiling water and salt in a small saucepan over medium heat and bring to a simmer. Place the wheat starch or cornflour and tapioca starch in the bowl of an electric mixer with a dough hook attachment and combine on low speed. Pour in the hot oil and water mixture in a steady stream and combine for 2 minutes until smooth. Cover the dough with plastic film and rest for 10 minutes at room temperature.

3 Preheat a large frying pan or wok over medium heat. Add the coconut oil and fry the snow pea shoots for 30 seconds, turning with tongs constantly to coat with the oil. Add the chives, shaohsing, soy sauce, salt and pepper, and leave to wilt for 30 seconds, then transfer to a bowl and set aside to cool.

4 Pinch off walnut-sized pieces of dough and roll them into balls, then into rounds about 10 cm in diameter and 2 mm thick. Place a teaspoon of filling in the centre and pinch or pleat the edges together to seal. Lightly oil a bamboo steamer and add the dumplings, working in batches or placing them over a couple of tiers. Cover with the lid and set over a saucepan of boiling water. Steam for 3–4 minutes or until opaque. Serve with the dipping sauce. ●

Serves 4

Pumpkin coconut curry

1 kg jap pumpkin, seeded and chopped into large chunks, skin on

2 tablespoons peanut oil

100 ml tamarind concentrate

1 teaspoon brown mustard seeds

1 cassia stick

2 green cardamom pods

2 large sprigs curry leaves

1½ onions, finely diced

2.5 cm ginger, peeled and grated

3 cloves garlic, chopped

5 small red chillies, chopped

2 large tomatoes, chopped

1 teaspoon chilli powder

1½ tablespoons ground coriander

1 teaspoon ground turmeric

2 teaspoons garam masala

1 × 400 ml tin coconut cream

1 tablespoon salt flakes

juice of 1 lemon or lime

basil leaves, to garnish

steamed jasmine rice, to serve

Marinade

1 tablespoon chilli powder

1 tablespoon ground coriander

1 teaspoon ground turmeric

1 teaspoon salt flakes

1 teaspoon black peppercorns, ground

juice of 1 lemon or lime

This dish is loosely based on a South Indian fish curry that was a long-standing menu item in a restaurant I worked in many years ago. The combination of coconut, chilli and fragrant spices with tamarind and lime is a favourite of mine. Here it balances out the sweetness of the cooked pumpkin, which I find a little cloying on its own. Peeling jap pumpkins is a culinary crime (although I'll make an exception if you are souping them). The skin is flavoursome and visually enticing, and it adds texture and structure. It also lowers the GI of the dish, as your body is designed to cope better when the available carbohydrate is buffered with naturally occurring fibre, like fruit with the skin on.

If you are feeling under-utilised in the kitchen, wash the seeds when you clean the pumpkin and roast them for a snack. Or, if you are feeling like a medicine man, you can blend them up into a thick goop and knock it back in the morning: the naturally occurring cucurbitins (amino acids) paralyse and, er, expunge, some intestinal parasites. I learnt this from the nicest farmers I know, Madeleine and Liam Burns, who are biodynamic wizards. They reckon this concoction has added benefits if combined with molasses and administered just shy of a full moon when gravitational forces are already having a 'pull' inside your body, making parasites wobbly. Hey, don't knock it: the moon can make the ocean rise and fall and we are made up of around 50 per cent water, so it makes sense . . .

1 To make the marinade, combine all the ingredients in a large bowl. Add the pumpkin and toss until well coated, then set aside for 30 minutes.

2 Heat the oil in a large heavy-based saucepan over medium–high heat. Working in batches, fry the marinated pumpkin for 4 minutes or so on each side, until browned all over. Remove the pumpkin from the pan and set aside.

3 Add 2 tablespoons of the tamarind concentrate to the pan and stir to lift the pumpkin residue. Add the mustard seeds, cassia, cardamom and curry leaves and fry, stirring, for 30 seconds until the mustard seeds start to pop (be careful not to let them burn as they will become bitter). Add the onion and fry, stirring, for 5 minutes or so until golden brown, then add the ginger, garlic, chopped chilli and tomato, and fry for about 10 minutes until the juices have evaporated. Add the chilli powder, coriander, turmeric and garam masala, and saute for about 5 minutes until the masala is aromatic and the raw ginger and garlic aromas have disappeared.

4 Add the coconut cream, 400 ml of water and the remaining tamarind concentrate to the pan and bring to a simmer. Add the salt and the fried pumpkin, stirring to combine. Cover and reduce the heat to low. Cook for 15 minutes or until the pumpkin is tender. Add the lemon or lime juice.

5 Sprinkle with basil leaves and serve with steamed jasmine rice. ◑

Steamed cumquat marmalade pudding

virgin coconut oil, for greasing

¼ cup (55 g) rapadura sugar

2 tablespoons pernod
or any anise liqueur

20 g lemon aspens
(or 2 tablespoons diced lime)

small handful of river mint
(or regular mint), finely chopped

pouring cream, to serve

Coconut pastry

1½ cups (225 g) self-raising
flour, sifted

⅔ cup (50 g) fresh
white breadcrumbs

1 tablespoon cumquat zest
(zest a couple of the cumquats
from the filling)

⅓ cup (80 g) virgin coconut oil

¼ cup (60 ml) cold milk

Filling

250 g cumquats, roughly chopped
into rounds and wedges
(pick out the seeds if you wish,
but I don't bother)

150 g unsalted butter,
cut into 5 mm dice

½ cup (110 g) rapadura sugar

pinch of ground lemon myrtle
(or lemon thyme leaves)

A great English dish, a Sussex pond is a steamed pudding traditionally made using suet dough with a whole skewered lemon and sugar placed inside. When the pudding is busted open, a slow ooze of citrus, pithiness and dense caramel leaks out like pond water. I really like the noise a steamed pudding makes rattling away on the stove and I love the finale of watching the liquid caramel weep like lava when you break into the pastry. Some versions omit the breadcrumbs in the dough but I like the added structure and texture. This version is for spring when my neighbourhood bustles with cumquats, sensational little fruit that almost always are left to drop. The native lemon aspens, spearmint-like river mint and lemon myrtle aren't essential and you can always use lime, regular mint and lemon thyme instead.

I am not an avoid-all-sugars-at-all-costs person. I use a variety of foods that are sweet, from sugar beets to honey to white sugar, but I mix them up and don't eat them often. In this recipe, I have thrown in the suggestion of rapadura sugar simply to get you thinking. You need sugar in the pudding and the choice of which one you use is yours but there are so many other options beyond white refined cane sugar. Rapadura is unrefined cane juice that is dried and ground. You could also try coconut palm sugar or just good old dark brown sugar, but the message is that less-refined sugars are probably a little better for you.

1 Preheat the oven to 190°C fan-forced (210°C conventional) and lightly grease a 14 cm round pudding bowl (about 8 cm deep) with coconut oil.

2 For the coconut pastry, place the flour, breadcrumbs, cumquat zest and coconut oil in a food processor and blitz until the mixture resembles breadcrumbs. In a small jug, combine the milk with ¼ cup (60 ml) of cold water. While the food processor is going, slowly add about ⅓ cup (80 ml) of the milk mixture to the flour mixture until it starts coming together as a dough. If the mixture seems dry, add a little more.

3 Turn out the dough onto a lightly floured benchtop and gently knead into a smooth ball. Take three-quarters of the pastry and roll it out to a thickness of about 5 mm (about 25 cm diameter), then line the base and side of the bowl. Roll out the remaining pastry to a thickness of about 5 mm (about 15 cm diameter) and place on a plate – this will be the lid. Pop the pastry-lined bowl and the pastry lid in the fridge for 30 minutes.

Steamed cumquat marmalade pudding
(cont.)

4 For the filling, place all the ingredients in a bowl and mix until well combined. Spoon the filling into the pastry-lined pudding bowl. Lightly brush the lid with water and place it on top, pressing the pastry edges together to seal. Cut out a 30 cm square of baking paper and cover it with foil. Fold a 2 cm pleat in the middle. Lightly oil the baking paper and place it over the pudding, oiled-side down. Crimp the edges together and seal the foil and paper with a couple of thick rubber bands or string.

5 Place an upside-down heatproof plate in a saucepan large enough to hold the pudding bowl. Place the bowl on top and carefully pour about 5 cm of boiling water into the saucepan, until the bowl is half submerged. Pop a lid on the saucepan, place over low heat and simmer for 1 hour. Remove the pudding from the heat and leave to stand for a couple of minutes.

6 Meanwhile, combine the sugar and liqueur with ⅓ cup (80 ml) of water in a small saucepan. Place over low heat and simmer for 5–7 minutes until syrupy, then remove from the heat and fold in the lemon aspens or lime.

7 Slide a small palette knife around the edge of the pudding bowl and invert quickly to release the pudding onto a serving plate. Garnish with mint and serve with the syrup and some chilled pouring cream. ●

Vietnamese cold noodle soup

250 g rice vermicelli noodles

1 iceberg lettuce, shredded

1 cup (80 g) bean sprouts

1 large carrot, peeled and cut into matchsticks

1 long cucumber, halved, seeded and cut into matchsticks

3 spring onions, green parts sliced

2 handfuls of coriander, cut into 2 cm lengths

handful of mint leaves

small handful of Vietnamese mint leaves

¼ cup (35 g) crushed roasted peanuts

Nuoc cham sauce

⅓ cup (80 ml) lime juice

¼ cup (65 g) coconut palm sugar

100 ml coconut water

¼ cup (60 ml) Thai-seasoned soy sauce (see page 36)

2 bird's eye chillies, finely sliced

3 cloves garlic, crushed

¼ teaspoon cracked white pepper

There are a few dishes I will eat no matter how tired or hot I am: hot and sour soup, gado gado and this Vietnamese cold soup. I always have herbs in the garden and in summer I'm lucky enough to have a well-shaded spot that gets filtered light and plenty of water. This means I can pop out the back door and fill a bucket with fistfuls of the three herbs that make this soup so special: coriander, mint and Vietnamese mint. It's a combination that is refreshing, interesting and harmonious.

The Vietnamese are masters of balance in their cooking and the sweet, hot, sour and herbaceous profile of this soup makes eating a bowl of it akin to plunging into a pool on a hot day – it leaves you totally revitalised. It goes without saying you need super-fresh lettuce and cucumber. As with all great yet simple dishes, there is no place for substandard ingredients to hide and escape scrutiny.

For a real hit of perfume, crack a fresh coconut for the coconut water in the nuoc cham sauce and it will lift the entire dish. And while we're on the subject, this is just a reminder that coconut palm sugar is a sustainable and renewable crop, unlike the palmyra plant, the harvesting of which is responsible for mass deforestation and the destruction of orang-utan habitat. Seek out producers who care.

1 Place the noodles in a large bowl and cover with hot water. Leave to soak for 10 minutes, then drain. Divide the noodles among six bowls.

2 For the nuoc cham sauce, place the lime juice and palm sugar in a jug and stir until the sugar dissolves. Add the coconut water, soy sauce, chilli, garlic and pepper, along with 200 ml of water. Stir until well combined.

3 Evenly divide the lettuce, bean sprouts, carrot, cucumber, spring onion, herbs and peanuts among the bowls of noodles.

4 Pour the nuoc cham sauce over the top and serve. ◗

Squash, taleggio
AND quinoa balls

2 tablespoons olive oil

1 large onion, finely diced

3 cloves garlic, crushed

1 cup (190 g) quinoa
(see Ingredients), rinsed

½ cup (40 g) quinoa flakes
(see Ingredients)

1 large spring onion, thinly sliced

200 g yellow squash, peeled
and cut into 4 mm dice

small handful of chopped
flat-leaf parsley

¼ teaspoon chilli flakes

½ cup (40 g) finely
grated parmesan

salt flakes and cracked
black pepper

100 g taleggio,
cut into 1 cm cubes

1 cup (150 g) plain flour

2 free-range eggs, lightly beaten

2 cups (140 g) fresh breadcrumbs

vegetable oil, for deep-frying

lemon wedges, to serve

I've long liked the idea of yellow squash, those cute little guys that look like they're wearing the iconic Canarinho strip of the Brazilian football team. However, I have tarnished memories of them from the '80s, cooked to death and served with tomato sauce, wrinkled, watery and frankly a little underwhelming. So, until recently, I'd always pick them up in the market in summer, entranced by their appearance, only to pop them right back down. That is until I decided to work with, instead of against, this watery characteristic.

I was angling for arancini using quinoa instead of rice when I cooked these up the first time. Quinoa flakes were nice and gluggy and bound everything up well, but became monotonous, a bit like a bowl of porridge. I added quinoa seeds for a welcome texture relief, but the mixture was still a little dry. Enter the squash – tada! – for it gives the whole thing a much-needed juicy boost.

1 Heat the olive oil in a heavy-based saucepan over low heat. Add the onion and garlic and fry for 10 minutes until the onion is translucent. Add the quinoa, quinoa flakes and 2 cups (500 ml) of water and increase the heat to high. Bring to a simmer, then reduce the heat to medium–low, cover and cook for 8 minutes. Remove from the heat and leave for 5 minutes, then uncover and leave for a further 10 minutes to help any excess liquid to evaporate.

2 Transfer the quinoa mixture to a large bowl and add the spring onion, squash, parsley, chilli and parmesan along with 1 teaspoon of salt and ½ teaspoon of pepper. Mix until well combined. Cover and leave for 30 minutes to firm up.

3 Shape the quinoa mixture into golfball-sized balls and insert a taleggio cube into the centre of each one. Place them on a large baking tray and leave to chill in the fridge for a couple of hours.

4 Place the flour in a shallow bowl and season with salt and pepper. Place the beaten eggs in a second bowl and the breadcrumbs in a third. Roll each quinoa ball in the flour, then dip in the egg and finally coat with the breadcrumbs. Return to the tray and refrigerate until required.

5 Pour the vegetable oil into a large heavy-based saucepan until a third full and heat over medium–high until just shimmering. Working in batches, deep-fry the balls for 3–5 minutes or until crisp and golden brown, then drain on paper towel. Serve with a sprinkle of salt and a good squeeze of lemon. ◖

Fig AND caramelised onion pizza WITH rocket

4 figs, quartered

120 g gorgonzola dolce

mint leaves, to garnish

large handful of baby rocket

⅓ cup (80 ml) extra virgin olive oil

salt flakes and cracked
black pepper

Caramelised onion

¼ cup (60 ml) olive oil

2 large onions, chopped

2 tablespoons brown sugar

2 tablespoons balsamic vinegar

4 sprigs thyme, leaves picked
and chopped

salt flakes and cracked
black pepper

Dough

1 teaspoon dried yeast

1 cup (150 g) plain flour

1 cup (160 g) wholemeal flour

1 teaspoon salt flakes

2 teaspoons extra virgin olive oil

coarse semolina, for sprinkling

To live with a fig tree in your garden is a surefire way of feeling privileged every day of summer. The fruit evokes images of luxury and in my mind a little bit of mystery and decadence. It keeps its flowers hidden on the inside, making it the most modest fruit on the planet. Figs look pretty enough as they ripen but you know they are hiding treasure under that layer of skin. This just kills me, as I am waiting for them to fatten and weep a little sappy juice to let me know they are ready. As agricultural cultivation of figs predates lentils and wheat, I think this is proof our ancestors could also be a little waggish and indulgent, perhaps just as captivated by this majestical fruit as I am.

Bottom heat is essential for a good pizza. No need for a trip to a fancy kitchen supply shop though; just grab an untreated paving stone, preheat it well and roll the dough nice and thin for best results.

1 For the dough, combine the yeast and 1 cup (250 ml) of lukewarm water in a small jug and stir well. Leave for 10 minutes until it begins to froth.

2 Combine the flours and salt in the bowl of an electric mixer with a dough hook, and mix until well combined. Add the yeast mixture and olive oil and mix on low speed to bring the dough together. Increase the speed to medium and knead for 6 minutes until the dough is smooth and elastic and clinging to the hook. (Alternatively, if making by hand, place the ingredients in a large bowl, bring together with your hands and turn out onto a lightly floured benchtop. Knead for about 8 minutes, turning the dough 90 degrees every fourth knead.) Place the dough in an oiled bowl and cover with plastic film. Leave to rise in a warm place for about an hour or until doubled in size.

3 Meanwhile, for the caramelised onion, heat the olive oil in a saucepan over low heat. Add the onion and fry for 2–3 minutes, then add the sugar, vinegar and thyme and season with salt and pepper. Fry for about 15 minutes or until the onion is caramelised. Remove from the heat and allow to cool.

4 Preheat the oven to 230°C fan-forced (250°C conventional). Lightly oil two 30 cm pizza trays (or use a pizza stone) and sprinkle with coarse semolina. Knock out the air from the dough and divide it in two. Oil your hands and work the dough as thinly as possible over the pizza trays, stretching, pushing and patting. Leave to rest for 5 minutes, then spread the onion over the top.

5 Bake the pizzas for 15 minutes, then reduce the temperature to 180°C fan-forced (200°C conventional). Remove the pizzas from the oven and lift them off their trays. Top with the figs and gorgonzola, then return the pizzas to the oven and bake for a further 2 minutes until the bases are crisp and the edges are golden. To serve, scatter with mint and rocket, drizzle with olive oil and season with salt and pepper. ◖

Radishes WITH labne, chickpeas AND mint

500 g Greek-style yoghurt

salt flakes

1 cup (200 g) dried kabuli chickpeas (see Ingredients), soaked overnight in cold water

bouquet garni

160 ml extra virgin olive oil

2 medium or 3 baby watermelon radishes, stems removed, shaved or thinly sliced (skins and all)

2 medium or 3 baby red radishes, stems removed, shaved or thinly sliced (skins and all)

grated zest and juice of 1 lemon

10 sprigs thyme, leaves picked and chopped

handful of mint leaves, torn

½ teaspoon cracked black pepper

Apologies in advance for the gender delineation – yeah, yeah, I know girls can barbecue and guys can make cupcakes – but placing this dish on the table makes me feel like I am channelling an uber-stylish lady who holds lunch parties complete with crisp linen napkins. I guess the vibrant pinks and creams are the culprits: they make this look so whimsical and pretty, like the breezy stuff of glossy lifestyle mags. It is, however, a dish of great flavour and substance.

The chickpeas are infused with a hint of aromatics in the form of a bouquet garni, a classic French blend of bay, thyme, rosemary, peppercorns, sometimes savory and nearly always parsley stalks. No need to buy one: just bundle the herbs and spices up and pop them in the cooking water. You can skip the traditional method of putting the peppercorns inside a celery stalk or leek sheaf, piling the herbs over the top and tying it all together with string by simply ramming the lot into a tea infuser. But this feels a little clinical to me and I like to think of all the great classic chefs who have tied a bouquet over the centuries. It's my way of giving a nod to those old masters by making sure tradition is honoured, even if it is a bit fiddly. It's nice to feel like you're a part of something timeless, that you belong to a craft or guild composed of a cast of thousands – cooks.

1 To make the labne, combine the yoghurt and 1 teaspoon of salt and mix well. Line a sieve with two pieces of muslin cloth and place over a bowl. Pour the yoghurt mixture into the centre of the lined sieve, then bring the edges of the cloth together and tie up to enclose. Place the labne (in the sieve over the bowl) in the fridge for at least 12 hours.

2 Drain the chickpeas and rinse them well, discarding the soaking water. Place them in a saucepan and cover with cold water by about 6 cm. Add the bouquet garni. Place over medium heat and simmer for about 1 hour or until the chickpeas are tender. Drain the chickpeas, then return them to the saucepan with 2 tablespoons of olive oil and ½ teaspoon of salt, tossing to combine. Leave to cool to room temperature.

3 Place the radishes in a bowl and dress with the lemon juice, remaining olive oil and a pinch of salt.

4 In a small bowl, mix the labne and thyme until well combined.

5 Spoon the chickpeas onto plates. Arrange the dressed radishes and a dollop of labne on top, then scatter with lemon zest, mint and pepper.

Black lentil, tomato AND kidney bean dal

½ cup (100 g) dried kidney beans, soaked overnight in cold water

¾ cup (150 g) black gram lentils (see Ingredients), soaked overnight in cold water

120 g butter

1 tablespoon grated ginger

2 cloves garlic, crushed

2 tomatoes, chopped

2 large green chillies, sliced

¼ cup (60 ml) tomato paste (puree)

2 teaspoons salt flakes

1 teaspoon chilli powder

¼ teaspoon ground cloves

2 cardamom pods

1 bay leaf

½ teaspoon ground cinnamon

⅔ cup (160 ml) pouring cream

small handful of coriander, chopped

Wholemeal flatbreads (see page 24) or Roti (see page 196) or basmati rice, to serve

To my mind this is the absolute king of all dals. You may have tried the dish in a Punjab restaurant and noticed a hint of delightful smokiness and wondered how on earth it got in there. Well, there is a little trick if you want to make this not just the best dal in the world but the best meal in the world full-stop. It's a showstopper yet really quite a simple method – and a lot of fun.

Grab a small piece of charcoal, pop it on a gas flame and get it hot enough to show some embers glowing. Meanwhile, peel an onion and hollow out the centre with a paring knife by cutting away about half of the middle rings but leaving a base: imagine you are making a bowl. When the dal has finished cooking, float the onion in the middle of the pan. Use tongs to place the charcoal inside the onion and then pour just half a teaspoon of ghee over the top and slam the lid on. The coal will start burning the onion flesh, the ghee will smoke like crazy and a rich smokiness will be imparted into the dal within a minute or two. The addition of woody spices (cardamom, cinnamon) in the ghee infuses some extra complexity but I usually don't bother. There you have it, my most coveted piece of lentil sorcery. Give it a shot and be both amazed and forewarned that you will be totally and utterly addicted to this dish forever after.

1 Drain the kidney beans and rinse them well, then place them in a saucepan with 400 ml of water. Bring to the boil over medium heat, then reduce the heat and simmer for 30 minutes. Drain the lentils and add them to the pan. Simmer for a further 30 minutes or until the kidney beans and lentils are tender. Drain and set aside.

2 Melt the butter in a large heavy-based saucepan or deep frying pan over medium heat. Add the ginger and garlic and fry for 2 minutes, then add the chopped tomato, green chilli, tomato paste, salt, chilli powder, cloves, cardamom, bay leaf and cinnamon. Cook for 10 minutes, then add the beans and lentils. Pour in 100 ml of cream and cook for a further 10–15 minutes, stirring occasionally. Add a little water if it becomes too dry.

3 Serve the dal hot, garnished with the remaining cream and the coriander, and accompanied by Indian bread or basmati rice. ●

Grape, gooseberry
AND spiced nut salad

60 g sultanas

2 tablespoons verjuice

1 cup (160 g) mixed nuts
(almonds, hazelnuts, pistachios,
walnuts, whatever you have)

1 tablespoon olive oil

100 g seedless grapes,
some halved

½ cup (40 g) cape gooseberries,
lanterns removed, or regular
gooseberries, halved

1 green apple, quartered,
cored and sliced

large handful of rocket

1 teaspoon walnut oil

salt flakes

Spice mix

½ teaspoon smoked paprika

1 teaspoon coriander seeds

½ teaspoon ground cassia bark

¼ teaspoon allspice

3 cloves

10 green cardamom seeds
(not pods)

This salad is made up of lots of little things that together deliver a big flavour. Cape gooseberries are another one of those whacked-out fruits that I love, not just for their tartness but for their crazy little paper lanterns. As they are ripening, the lantern dries out a bit and they resemble an intricately wrapped present. In this dish, they play particularly well with the sweet, juicy grapes. Feel free to use normal gooseberries as a substitute.

Nuts at this time of the year need a good toast, as they have been sitting around since autumn. Here they are well toasted and then shallow-fried, which may seem excessive but it really does bring them back to life. The walnut oil should be used sparingly as it can overpower other ingredients and bring a cloying element to the dish.

Seasonal purists will just have to close their eyes when they see apple in the ingredients. I just love apple and nuts and they give this salad some much-needed crispness. I won't bite into a cold-stored apple as a snack but in this context I reckon they are absolutely fine.

1 To make the spice mix, use a mortar and pestle to grind all the ingredients to a coarse powder.

2 Place the sultanas in a small bowl. Warm the verjuice in a small saucepan, then pour it over the sultanas. Leave for 15 minutes to allow the sultanas to soften and plump up.

3 Place the nuts in a dry heavy-based frying pan over medium–high heat and lightly toast them, moving them regularly so they don't burn. Add the spice mix and fry for a couple of minutes until aromatic. Add the olive oil and fry for a further 1–2 minutes, then remove from the heat and allow to cool.

4 In a serving bowl, combine the grapes, gooseberries, apple, rocket, sultanas and spiced nuts, tossing to combine. Drizzle over the walnut oil, season with salt and toss again to combine. Serve immediately. ◖

Baked eggplant skins <u>WITH</u> babaganoush, red lentils <u>AND</u> polenta

¾ cup (150 g) red nugget lentils
(or other medium unhulled
red lentils; see Ingredients)

¼ cup (60 ml) extra virgin olive oil

2 medium eggplants (aubergines)

2 tablespoons unhulled tahini

2 tablespoons Greek-style yoghurt

2 tablespoons lemon juice

salt flakes and cracked
black pepper

1 tablespoon grated lemon zest

handful of flat-leaf parsley leaves

Polenta

2 cups (500 ml) milk

100 g coarse polenta

1 teaspoon salt flakes

50 g butter, cubed

¾ cup (60 g) grated parmesan

This recipe calls for red nugget lentils because they are earthy and robust, plus they grow well in Australia and are readily available. The huge smoky eggplant flavour and cheesy polenta will simply stomp over a delicate variety of lentil, but nuggets are tough little guys that can stand up to the bold flavours in this dish. Any mid-sized red lentil will do, but I am a lentil fanatic and if meat recipes can call for a certain breed and cut, I reckon it's about time we started taking lentils seriously too. We can at least start naming the different varieties – after all, they each have their own unique properties and place in cooking. (Oh, and I can hear you saying, 'But they look brown in the picture!' Have a read of the Ingredients section to become lentil-literate. Lentils are more often than not named by seed, not skin, colour.)

This is one of the punchiest vegie recipes in my repertoire, one I'll gladly serve to a big, burly carnivore. In fact, the (inauthentic) addition of yoghurt to the babaganoush is precisely because the dish really needs something to lighten it up – testament to how full-on and brash vegies can be.

1 Place the lentils and 3 cups (750 ml) of water in a saucepan. Bring to the boil over high heat, then reduce the heat to medium–low and simmer for 40 minutes or until the lentils are just tender and nestled in a small amount of water. (Top up the water if the lentils become too dry, but keep the liquid level low or the lentils will lose flavour.) Set aside.

2 Meanwhile, preheat the oven to 180°C fan-forced (200°C conventional). Take two 30 cm squares of foil and lightly brush them with olive oil. Place an eggplant in the centre of each square and wrap them up like baked spuds. Bake the eggplants for about 40 minutes or until they are lovely and mushy. Remove from the oven, open up the foil and leave to cool for 10 minutes. Halve the eggplants and gently remove the flesh, reserving the skins. Place the flesh in a food processor with the tahini, yoghurt and lemon juice and season well with salt. Pulse until well combined.

3 For the polenta, bring the milk and 2 cups (500 ml) of water to a steady simmer. Rain in the polenta, whisking continuously. Reduce the heat to low and add the salt, then cook for 25 minutes, stirring to prevent sticking. Fold in the butter and parmesan, then divide the polenta among plates.

4 Place the eggplant skins on the polenta and spoon in the babaganoush. Add the lentils and some of their juice, then drizzle olive oil over the top and season with salt and pepper. Serve sprinkled with lemon zest and parsley. ◗

Serves 4

500 g silken tofu, sliced into
1 cm thick pieces

1 teaspoon ground sichuan pepper

⅓ cup (80 ml) peanut oil

small handful of coriander leaves

steamed jasmine rice, to serve

Dressing

1 tablespoon finely chopped ginger

2 tablespoons sliced spring onion

2 tablespoons chopped
coriander stems

2 tablespoons Chinese
dark soy sauce (or any dark soy)

2 tablespoons Chinese
black vinegar (see page 61)

1½ tablespoons light soy sauce

1 tablespoon sesame oil

¼ teaspoon chilli oil (see below)

Chilli oil

1 large red chilli, roughly chopped,
seeds and all

pinch of salt flakes

2 tablespoons vegetable oil

Steamed then seared tofu WITH fresh chilli oil

I love this method. Steaming the silken tofu creates an interesting texture, then searing it with hot oil brings all the aromas of the sauce to life. The absolute hero of the dish, however, is the sichuan pepper, which I find numbing, warming and almost medicinal in taste. Tasmanian mountain pepper has a very similar flavour profile, so if you can get hold of some, try using it instead – it bleeds a magnificent dark purple hue into the bowl when the searing oil hits it. Like sichuan pepper, which comes from the prickly ash shrub, it is not a true or vine peppercorn but rather a tree pepper and named thus because of its pungent pepper-like heat. Cuisine-specific soy sauces (Chinese, Thai and Japanese) have slightly different flavours. Any dark soy will do here though: it's better to get the style right (light or dark) rather than the country of origin.

Here's a top gardening tip, too: you can make your own bug spray with the leftover chilli from the chilli oil. Mix it up with 2 teaspoons of crushed garlic, ½ teaspoon of pounded fennel seeds, 1 teaspoon of olive oil, ½ teaspoon of soap flakes and 1 litre of water. Let it sit for a few days, then shake it up and pop it in a spray bottle. It's brilliant stuff for keeping white flies, aphids, snails and caterpillars away from the vegie patch.

1 To make the chilli oil, pound all the ingredients using a mortar and pestle to make a paste. Place in a fine sieve and press with the back of a spoon to extract the oil. Discard the solids (or use it in a bug spray – see intro!).

2 Bring a large saucepan of water to the boil over medium heat. Lightly oil a bamboo steamer, add the tofu and cover with the lid. Set the steamer over the saucepan and steam the tofu for 8–10 minutes.

3 Meanwhile, for the dressing, mix all the ingredients together, stirring until well combined. Set aside.

4 Divide the steamed tofu among small bowls or deep plates. Pour over the dressing and sprinkle with ⅛ to ¼ teaspoon of sichuan pepper per serve, depending on how hot you like it.

5 In a very small saucepan, heat the peanut oil over medium–high until smoking. Do not leave the oil unattended – you have a very small window before it ignites. Carefully pour the smoking-hot oil over the dressed tofu.

6 Garnish with coriander and serve with steamed jasmine rice. ●

Mango AND maca rice puffs

¼ cup (30 g) chia seeds

40 g puffed brown rice

100 g dried mango, cut into 1 cm pieces

¼ cup (25 g) goji berries

1 cup (75 g) shredded coconut

2 tablespoons maca powder

grated zest of 1 orange

60 g cocoa butter

180 g honey

2 vanilla beans, split and seeds scraped

Periodically craving fat and sugar is hardwired into our brains. Most natural sugars come in packages that contain other nutrients and/or ample fibre to buffer their uptake into our bloodstream. Likewise, in nature, most fats are not easy to find and are bundled up with proteins and vitamins and minerals. So I say it doesn't hurt to have a moderate intake of the good sugars and fats and these little energy balls are delicious. I suggest you seek out some sulphur-free naturally dried mango, as the discolouration from processing without sulphur is minimal and the flavour is so much better. Most of the natural stuff will have the added benefit of being fairly recently processed too.

When it comes to honey, the cooler the extraction process, the more natural it is. Low-temperature extracted honeys will always be slightly candied; I like to see a few bits floating around in the jar as proof of minimal filtering. Our Australian honey is some of the best in the world and I love the complex, deep-flavoured stuff made by bees collecting from robust flora. Some of the more refined imported honeys just taste like glucose to me – perhaps unsurprisingly when some of them are derived from bees actually fed on liquid sugars rather than the abundance of nectar we have in this country.

The shopping list for these rice puffs is pretty straightforward and a trip to a decent health food shop should see it ticked off. I am, however, reluctant to call any of the ingredients 'superfoods'. Bah – all food is superfood as long as it is pretty close to the form and quantity that nature provides.

1 Soak the chia seeds in ½ cup (125 ml) of water for at least 30 minutes until the seeds have absorbed all the liquid.

2 In a large bowl, combine the puffed rice, dried mango, goji berries, coconut, maca powder and orange zest. Stir until well combined.

3 Melt the cocoa butter in a small saucepan over low heat, then add the honey and vanilla seeds. Stir until runny. Pour this over the rice mixture, then add the soaked chia seeds and stir until everything is well coated.

4 Roll the mixture into golfball-sized balls, pressing the ingredients together to bind. Place on a plate and leave to set at room temperature for 1 hour. These can be stored in an airtight container for up to 2 weeks. ●

Chargrilled strawberry AND rocket salad WITH pita

500 g strawberries,
hulled and halved

⅓ cup (80 ml) olive oil

2 tablespoons balsamic vinegar

1 tablespoon chopped tarragon

½ teaspoon salt flakes

½ teaspoon cracked black pepper

200 g wholemeal pita bread

50 g wild rocket (it may be
flowering in summer – bonus!)

½ red onion, finely sliced

⅔ cup (110 g) toasted and lightly
crushed almonds

handful of mint leaves, torn

handful of basil leaves, torn

When you have done everything you can with strawberries – enjoyed new-season ones fresh, baked with them, chucked them on your yoghurt or cereal every morning, made jam – then it's time to throw a few on the barbecue. This method is perfect for 'imperfect' fruit, the end-of-season stuff that isn't pristine.

Tarragon, black pepper and strawberry with a touch of vinegar is a (polygamous) marriage that sees the fruit pushed to a whole new level. And once they are smoked up on the grill, they are ready to fight it out with the wild rocket. I say this because wild rocket is unapologetically peppery and robust, nothing like its broad-leaved relative. The latter is pleasant but, let's face it, it's the rocket you have when you don't really want rocket!

1 Place the strawberries in a large bowl and add the olive oil, vinegar, tarragon, salt and pepper. Toss to combine, then leave to macerate for 10 minutes.

2 Meanwhile, preheat a grill to high and toast the pita on both sides. Leave to cool, then rip it up and place it in a large bowl with the rocket, onion, almonds, mint and basil, tossing until well combined.

3 Heat a chargrill pan over medium–high heat. Fish the strawberries out, reserving the marinade. Chargrill them for 3–4 minutes, kicking them around a bit to colour all sides. Remove from the heat and allow to cool.

4 Add the strawberries and the reserved marinade to the salad and toss to combine. Transfer to a serving dish and serve immediately. ◑

Radish pod, white pepper AND garlic stir-fry

1 bunch coriander, leaves picked, stems and roots rinsed

6 cloves garlic, roughly chopped

1 teaspoon white peppercorns

pinch of salt flakes

½ cup (125 ml) flavour-neutral oil (see page 33)

125 g radish pods or sugar snaps

250 g snow peas (mange tout)

250 g bean sprouts or soy sprouts

3 cm ginger, peeled and cut into fine matchsticks

¼ teaspoon white sugar

⅓ cup (80 ml) Thai-seasoned soy sauce (see page 36)

steamed jasmine rice, to serve

Missing a little 'pop' in your food? Well, you need to grow some radishes and leave one or two in the ground. Once the weather warms up, they will bolt and the resulting seedpods are testament to how not boring vegies are. Rat's tail radishes are often grown just for this purpose, but the giant Japanese daikon will produce a similar little seedpod. Pick them when they are a couple of centimetres long, before they become woody, and get busy in the wok. They produce a gentle radish burn when you bite into them; they are also surprisingly full of air (as well as the pea-like seed) and make for a unique texture.

Some fancy 'vegeteers' sell these radish pods in early summer, but if you can't get them or grow them, just substitute sugar snap peas. The dish is still brilliant and the requisite warmth derived from the radish pods will not be terribly missed as the finely sliced ginger provides a gentle zing. And yes, I made the word 'vegeteers' up but there are some amazing little niche growers and distributors. A shout-out goes to Rachel McMillan from Scoop on South Australia's Fleurieu Peninsula, who painstakingly gathered pods for this cookbook shoot. She always has something interesting on her weekly mailout of produce grown with love. On ya, Rach xxx

1 Using a mortar and pestle, pound the coriander roots and stems, garlic, peppercorns and salt to a smooth paste.

2 Place a wok over high heat and add the oil. Once shimmering, add the paste and fry for 30 seconds or until aromatic. Add the radish pods or sugar snaps, snow peas, sprouts, ginger and sugar, tossing well to combine. Fry for 1–2 minutes, then add the soy sauce and 100 ml of water. Cook for a further minute, then remove the wok from the heat. Add the coriander leaves and toss to combine.

3 Serve the stir-fry with steamed jasmine rice. ◗

445 g shortcrust pastry,
thawed if frozen, brought
to room temperature

30 g butter

¼ cup (35 g) plain flour

1½ cups (375 ml) cold milk

1 bay leaf

1 bunch asparagus, trimmed
and chopped into 1 cm pieces

6 sprigs tarragon, leaves picked

½ cup (60 g) grated gruyere

salt flakes and cracked
black pepper

6 free-range eggs

Asparagus, tarragon AND baked egg tarts

Tarragon and egg, egg and asparagus, asparagus and tarragon: it doesn't matter which way you pair these ingredients they just work, and all three together is pure harmony. For best results, make sure your blind-baked pastry shell and your filling mixture are a similar temperature. Most recipes call for a cold shell and a cold mix but I find if both are warm the result is just as good; it's when there is a difference in temperatures that you end up with the dreaded soggy bottom. Speaking of textures, I am also slightly pedantic when baking eggs. I always take them to the point where the white is set and the yolk still runny. Perfectly baked eggs combined with crisp pastry and a smooth bechamel sauce make this one of my favourite breakfasts or suppers.

I always look for young, delicate asparagus for these tarts. If your asparagus is a little woody, you may have to give it a quick blanch before popping it in the sauce. I am always being told off for fondling the food in the market but wrinkles on otherwise smooth stems, discolouration where the knife has cut off the base and mushy tips are all signs the asparagus has hung around a little too long after picking. I am prepared to get my hands slapped by a few vendors if it means getting up close and personal with produce. It's a small price to pay to get the best.

1 Lightly grease a large 6-hole muffin tin or 6 large baking foils. On a lightly floured benchtop, roll the pastry until it is 3 mm thick, then cut out six 15 cm rounds. Line the prepared tin or foils with the pastry, then place in the fridge for 30 minutes.

2 Preheat the oven to 190°C fan-forced (210° conventional).

3 Melt the butter in a small saucepan over medium–low heat. Add the flour and cook, stirring, for 1–2 minutes to cook out the flour. Add the milk slowly, whisking continuously to prevent lumps, then add the bay leaf and slowly bring to a simmer. Cook for 5 minutes or until the sauce has thickened. Stir in the asparagus, most of the tarragon (reserve a little to garnish) and half of the gruyere, then season with salt and pepper. Remove from the heat and set aside at room temperature. Discard the bay leaf.

4 Line each pastry case with baking paper and fill with baking beans or rice. Blind-bake for 15 minutes, then remove the paper and beans and return the pastry to the oven for a further 5 minutes or until just set but not coloured.

5 Evenly divide the warm asparagus mixture among the pastry shells. Crack an egg on top of each one and sprinkle over the remaining gruyere. Return the tarts to the oven and bake for a further 10–15 minutes or until the whites are set but the yolks are still runny. Garnish with tarragon and serve warm. ●

Serves 6

Tromboncino frittata

600 g tromboncino or
2 large zucchini (courgettes)

2 tablespoons olive oil

1 clove garlic, crushed

grated zest of 1 lemon

1 tablespoon chopped mint

2 tablespoons chopped
flat-leaf parsley

6 free-range eggs, lightly beaten

2 cups (500 ml) pouring cream

½ teaspoon salt flakes

¼ teaspoon cracked black pepper

100 g feta, crumbled

Tromboncini, whacky-looking members of the squash family with pale green skins, arrive in summer. They can be left to mature into autumn but the skins become a little brown and tough and then they are more suited to roasting. Summer tromboncini are waxy and juicy, with a hint of avocado creaminess. Regular zucchini will still work in this dish but they lack this butteriness, so I urge you to hunt down a tromboncino and give it a whirl.

On that note, this frittata looks quite literally like a whirlwind, with the tromboncino pieces creating a spiral in the pan. They peek out of the egg mix and you end up with crispy brown bits on top and creamy bits where they are submerged. If you use regular zucchini, just use a little less egg mix but be careful not to make the frittata so thin that it becomes an omelette.

1 Lightly oil a large non-stick frying pan with a heatproof handle (about 25 cm diameter is good). Using a mandolin, slice the tromboncino or zucchini lengthways into strips and place in a large bowl. In a small jug, whisk together the olive oil, garlic, lemon zest, mint and parsley until combined. Pour over the tromboncino or zucchini strips and toss to coat well.

2 Roll a strip of the dressed tromboncino or zucchini into a tight circle. Then, wrap another strip around it, followed by another strip, allowing a little room for the egg mix to penetrate between the layers later. Repeat this process until you have a 10 cm diameter spiral, then place it in the centre of the frying pan. Repeat with the remaining tromboncino or zucchini until all of the strips have been used or until you have reached the edge of the pan and can't fit any more spirals in.

3 In a small bowl, whisk together the eggs, cream, salt and pepper until well combined. Carefully pour the egg mixture over the spirals in the pan, then sprinkle over the feta. Place the frying pan over medium–low heat and cook the frittata for 8 minutes or until it is set around the edge but still runny in the centre.

4 Preheat the grill to medium–high. Place the frying pan under the preheated grill for 5 minutes or until the frittata is golden brown and just set. Remove and allow to cool for 5 minutes before turning out onto a serving plate.

Chargrilled cos WITH blue cheese AND borlotti beans

500 g fresh young borlotti beans, in pods (250 g podded)

juice of 1 lemon

2 tablespoons chopped flat-leaf parsley

⅓ cup (80 ml) olive oil

salt flakes and cracked black pepper

1 baby red cos, halved

1 baby green cos, halved

2 tablespoons aged red wine vinegar

160 g blue cheese (gorgonzola or dolce latte are good), crumbled

Borlotti beans have a really short season in mid to late summer. If you have eaten them fresh, you will know that for very little effort and time you get spectacular eating. The pods have a deep magenta hue and cream flecks; the beans are decorated in an inverse fashion, being cream with little flecks of red detail that look almost hand painted. They seem to be dressed up and ready for a catwalk show – definitely the visual stars of the summer vegetable season.

Don't be afraid of destroying the cos hearts in the pan here. We are so conditioned not to burn food that it is counterintuitive to hang in there a little longer while the cos gets sadder and sadder. But the flavour that develops is worth it. I prefer the sweeter blue cheese varieties for this dish as they play nicely with the cos, but a sharp blue is fine if that's your thing.

I will travel far and wide to get good vinegar. The balance of acidity and sweetness is part of the deal, but lingering notes and flavours that come on slowly are something else to consider. You should be able to drink a tablespoon of decent vinegar without pulling a nasty face, then feel a little rush through your nose and taste a pleasant acidity washing over your palate, before finally be left pondering all the subtle woody and aromatic characteristics that remain for 30-odd seconds. If you wince and feel only pain, I suggest you move on spend a little for something that has been loved in the making.

1 Place the beans in a large saucepan and cover with salted water by about 5 cm. Bring to the boil, then reduce the heat and simmer for 20 minutes or until the beans are tender. Drain.

2 Transfer the beans to a bowl and stir through the lemon juice, parsley and 1 tablespoon of olive oil. Season with salt and pepper, and set aside.

3 Meanwhile, heat a chargrill pan over high heat. Drizzle the remaining olive oil over the halved cos and season with salt and pepper. Place them cut-side down in the pan and chargrill for 1–2 minutes or until golden and slightly charred. Turn over and cook for a further 1–2 minutes. Remove from the heat and place on serving plates.

4 Top the chargrilled cos with the dressed borlotti beans. To serve, drizzle over the vinegar and finish with the crumbled blue cheese. ◗

Goat's cheese, onion AND cognac tart WITH olives

300 g pearl or pickling onions (or golden shallots), skin on

2 cups (500 ml) extra virgin olive oil

2½ tablespoons cognac

salt flakes and cracked black pepper

375 g all-butter puff pastry, thawed if frozen, brought to room temperature

1 free-range egg, lightly beaten

50 g goat's cheese, crumbled

30 g dried salt-cured olives, pitted

1 tablespoon vincotto

2 tablespoons chopped chives

With their delicious chewiness and intensity of flavour, the dried olives are the standout in this tart. You'll find them in packets, sans liquid, looking like dried prunes only smaller. If you haven't tried them yet, this is the dish to test-drive them. Meanwhile, the goat's cheese brings a tang that cuts straight through the sweetness of the onions and vincotto. By all means use brandy instead of cognac, but the complex wood, fruit and floral notes simply shoot through the tart.

If you have flambe trepidation, as many cooks do – don't! Alcohol is not gunpowder. (That said, the navy apparently used to check that their ration of rum was not watered down by mixing it with gunpowder. If the gunpowder didn't ignite with a match, it was not 100 per cent proof, which I guess you need if you are mad enough to sail in a rickety boat getting shot at by cannons all the time.) Anyway, be reassured that the total available combustible material in this recipe equates to about a tablespoon, an amount that will burn off very quickly and be contained in the pan . . . Do you feel better now? If you are still a little flambe-frigid, then grab a flambe pot with a super-long handle. Oh, and always make sure you put on your best frock – if it goes terribly wrong, you might just meet a nice fireman.

1 Place the onions in a saucepan and pour over the olive oil. Place over low heat and cook very gently for 1 hour or until the skins are dark golden. Drain, reserving the oil. Leave the onions to cool, then peel off their skins. Place the onions and cognac in a large frying pan over medium heat. If cooking over gas, tip the pan slightly to ignite the alcohol or alternatively light with a match. Once the flame burns out (after a few seconds), remove from the heat. Place a quarter of the onions in a food processor with 2 tablespoons of the reserved oil. Blend to a paste, then season well.

2 Line a large baking tray with baking paper. On a lightly floured work surface, roll the pastry until it is about 3 mm thick, and about 35 cm × 15 cm. Cut around the edges – this will enable the pastry to puff properly – then place on the prepared tray. Using a sharp knife, gently score a 2 cm border, being careful not to cut all the way through. Using a fork, prick the centre of the pastry all over. Cover with plastic film and place in the fridge for 30 minutes.

3 Preheat the oven to 200°C fan-forced (220°C conventional). Brush the pastry border with the egg. Bake for 15 minutes until puffed and light golden, then remove from the oven and reduce the temperature to 180°C fan-forced (200°C conventional). Gently push the centre of the pastry down and spread with the onion paste. Top with the remaining onions, cheese and olives. Bake the tart for a further 10 minutes or until the cheese is golden and the onions are warm. Serve drizzled with vincotto and garnished with chives. ●

Indian hokkien mee

150 g starchy potatoes
(such as colibans, kennebecs
or russets)

salt flakes

200 g hokkien noodles

100 ml flavour-neutral oil
(see page 33)

2 free-range eggs

½ teaspoon sambal oelek

1 small onion, sliced

2 cloves garlic, crushed

pinch of sugar

¼ bunch Chinese broccoli,
stems sliced into 2 cm lengths,
leaves halved

75 ml good-quality tomato ketchup

1 tablespoon light soy sauce

1 tablespoon dark soy sauce

1 tablespoon kecap manis

2 small tomatoes, cut into wedges

⅔ cup (50 g) bean sprouts
(or soy or lentil sprouts)

1 tablespoon tamarind concentrate

2 handfuls of basil leaves

2 tablespoons roasted peanuts

lemon wedges, to serve

This dish is a great example of a cultural melting pot. An over-simplified rundown of events goes like this: Hokkien-speaking workers from the southern Chinese Fujian province who ended up in Singapore introduced this dish to the streets of Malaysia. The original Singaporean hokkien mee contained prawns and squid and was fried in pork fat; the Southern Indian Malaysians, the Mamaks, omitted the non-halal pork fat; the addition of ketchup is believed to be a British–Indian influence.

I have seen many slightly different variants of hokkien mee being cooked in the Brickfields district known as Little India just outside Kuala Lumpur. On my travels I'll often sit down to a bowl of hawker food, keeping one eye covertly on the kitchen, and try to work out what secret ingredient the chef is adding to the wok or pot. I'll always compliment the chef and attempt to pry some information from the secretive street vendors, usually to little avail. Luckily for me, I worked with a Mamak cook at one stage, so this version is my messed-up vegetarian adaptation of Bob's noodles. The addition of potato always used to mystify me and I know it sounds wrong, but I assure you it's a winning combination. The basil is there because it's abundant in summer and works brilliantly with the tomato and chilli.

Some people would argue that the dish needs true hokkien noodles, which are egg free. The signature yellow tinge comes from treating the wheat flour with an alkaline solution during the dough-making process. It gives the noodles their hue and a slippery but chewy texture. If you have the time and inclination, grab some lye water from an Asian grocer and get Googling. It's quite an easy process and brings a little kitchen surprise when the white dough magically turns yellow.

1 Place the potatoes in a saucepan and cover with water and a pinch of salt. Bring up to a simmer over medium heat and cook for 15–20 minutes until tender. Drain and leave to cool slightly, then break into golfball-sized pieces.

2 Bring a saucepan of water to the boil, add the noodles and blanch for 30 seconds. Drain well.

3 Heat the oil in a wok over high heat until shimmering. Crack the eggs into a shallow bowl and break the yolks using a wok tool or spatula, then gently slide them into the wok. Don't disturb the eggs at all – just leave them to cook for about a minute or until the whites are set, then slide them up the side of the wok. Add the sambal, onion and garlic and leave for 30 seconds until the onion has softened, then add the potato, noodles, sugar and broccoli and stir-fry for a minute or so until the broccoli stems have softened. Finally, add the ketchup, light soy, dark soy, kecap manis, tomato, sprouts, tamarind and a pinch of salt, and stir to combine. Serve garnished with basil and peanuts, with a lemon wedge for squeezing over.

Sour orange curry WITH Burmese tofu

8 dried red chillies, roughly chopped (seeds and all)

6 cm galangal, peeled and roughly chopped

½ tablespoon salt flakes

4 red shallots, roughly chopped

150 ml tamarind concentrate

1 teaspoon coconut palm sugar (see page 70)

140 ml Thai-seasoned soy sauce (see page 36)

250 g red and yellow cherry tomatoes, some halved

100 g green beans, halved

large handful of betel leaves or baby spinach, shredded

steamed jasmine rice, to serve

Burmese tofu

1 cup (150 g) chickpea (besan) flour

1 teaspoon salt flakes

½ teaspoon ground turmeric

Burmese tofu is made using chickpea (besan) flour. You can make tofu with chickpeas using a traditional soybean-based method and I love it, but this is a different, although equally delicious, type. It is made by cooking out a turmeric-seasoned besan-flour slurry and then setting it to a texture similar to silken tofu. Besan flour is ground-up chana dal or desi chickpea flour. The desi chickpea is the smaller, darker-yellow Indian legume, which is related to the larger and paler Afghan kabuli variety. In flour form, the two varieties have very different properties in relation to water ratios and setting strength. When shopping for ingredients, you're on the right track if the besan is yellow or light brown; if it looks a little white or cream I would skip it.

The method may seem confusing at first but letting the batter sit overnight allows two things to happen. Firstly, the starches swell and this is required for binding. Secondly, a thick layer of sludge forms in the bottom of the bowl with a more watery layer on top. Pouring the less-concentrated top layer into the boiling water first prevents clumping and you can then gradually add the thicker bottom layer. For some reason, the tofu just sets better using this method.

The curry itself is light, watery and similar to a hot and sour soup, with a pinch of sweetness from the coconut palm sugar, green beans and height-of-season lolly-sweet cherry tomatoes. It's exactly the sort of spicy dish that stimulates a sluggish appetite when the days are hot and long. Throwing the pounded aromatics and shallots in simmering water rather than frying them gives a distinct 'pure' flavour. It is a method not unlike infusing a stock and really leaves the galangal and chilli to sing.

1 For the Burmese tofu, sift the chickpea flour, salt and turmeric into a bowl and pour in 1½ cups (375 ml) of water, whisking continuously to make a smooth batter. Pass through a sieve if necessary to remove any lumps. For best results, leave the batter overnight at room temperature.

2 Line a baking tray with a clean cloth or muslin – this will help to absorb excess moisture. The size of the tray can vary but you want the length and width to add up to about 45 cm so, for example, a 25 cm × 20 cm tin would be fine, as would a 30 cm × 15 cm tin. It should be at least 3 cm deep. Bring 1½ cups (375 ml) of water to the boil in a wide and shallow heavy-based saucepan, then reduce the heat to medium. Gently pour the top watery layer of batter into the water in a steady stream, whisking continuously. Reduce the heat to medium–low and cook the gently bubbling batter for 5 minutes. Stream the remaining thicker batter into the pan, then reduce the heat to very low and cook for 20–30 minutes, scraping the bottom of the pan with a spatula to prevent burning. Watch it like a hawk – it's really sticky!

Sour orange curry WITH Burmese tofu (cont.)

3 Pour the tofu batter into the prepared tray and smooth the top. Fold over the edges of the cloth to enclose it, then place in the fridge for 1 hour, until firm. Carefully lift the tofu in its cloth out of the tray and place on a wire rack. Set the rack over the baking tray and leave in the fridge for at least 2 hours to drain (or for a firmer tofu, leave overnight).

4 An hour before you make the curry, bring the tofu up to room temperature. You'll need 500 g for this recipe; the rest can remain covered in the fridge for up to 5 days. If you set it overnight, it can also be deep-fried until golden.

5 Pound the chilli, galangal, salt and shallot to a paste using a mortar and pestle. Transfer to a large saucepan over medium heat and add the tamarind, sugar, soy sauce and 1.5 litres of water. Bring to the boil and cook for 5 minutes, then add the tomatoes and green beans. Cook for a further 2 minutes before adding the betel leaves or spinach.

6 Divide the curry among bowls and gently spoon the tofu on top. Serve with steamed jasmine rice. ◑

Coriander beancurd sticks WITH coconut bean sprout salad

125 g sweet beancurd sticks
(see Ingredients)

2 cups (400 g) sticky rice, soaked
overnight in cold water

½ small bunch coriander, stems
and roots rinsed, leaves reserved

3 cloves garlic, peeled

1 teaspoon white peppercorns

salt flakes

½ cup (135 g) coconut palm sugar
(see page 70)

⅓ cup (80 ml) light soy sauce

¾ cup (50 g) coriander seeds

1 cup (150 g) cornflour
(or use wheat starch; see page 61)

2 free-range egg whites

2 cups (500 ml) vegetable oil

Coconut bean sprout salad

2 tablespoons shredded
coconut, toasted

¼ cup (35 g) roasted
peanuts, crushed

2 cups (160 g) bean sprouts

2 small red shallots, sliced

handful of coriander leaves
(reserved from above)

½ cup (125 ml) coconut cream

2 tablespoons rice vinegar
or white wine vinegar

This is a vego approximation of a Thai road snack prepared by curing beef strips in soy and palm sugar with garlic, coriander roots and pepper. Essentially jerky with a few spices, it is then left in the sun to dry. When passers-by need a little something to eat, the strips are popped into a wok of shimmering oil. Sweet beancurd sticks have a great chewy texture but, like many soy products, they can be a little bland so the sweet soy marinade works wonders here.

Don't be alarmed at the amount of coriander seed in the crust. It is one of the few spices you can go crazy with as it harmonises all the flavours it accompanies. I never cook savoury sticky rice using the absorption method. Soaking it then steaming it allows it to be a little sticky but retain structure. This makes it the perfect accompaniment to the creamy sprout salad and chewy bean sticks.

1 Place the beancurd sticks in a bowl, cover with warm water and leave to soak for 30 minutes. Wrap the soaked sticks in a tea towel and press gently to squeeze out excess moisture. Place in a bowl and set aside.

2 Bring a saucepan of water to the boil over medium heat and set a steamer on top. Place a damp muslin cloth (or an old, clean tea towel) over the base of the steamer. Drain and rinse the rice, then place it in the steamer. Steam for 30 minutes, then set aside.

3 Use a mortar and pestle to crush the coriander stems and roots with the garlic, peppercorns and a little salt. Pound to a paste, then add the palm sugar and soy sauce. Pour over the bean sticks, tossing until well coated. Leave for 20 minutes to allow the flavours to infuse.

4 Coarsely crack the coriander seeds using a mortar and pestle or spice grinder. Go easy – you want them to remain in halves or quarters, so don't grind them to dust – then transfer to a shallow bowl. Place the wheat starch or cornflour in another bowl. Place the egg whites in a bowl and run a whisk through to froth them up a bit. Pull the bean sticks out of the marinade and dredge them through the starch or flour, shaking off any excess, then run them through the egg whites. Finally dredge them through the cracked coriander seeds, pressing well to coat.

5 For the coconut bean sprout salad, pound the coconut and peanuts to a coarse paste using a mortar and pestle. Place the bean sprouts, shallots and coriander leaves in a serving bowl, add the paste and toss together to combine. Add the coconut cream and vinegar, and toss to coat.

6 Heat the oil in a wok over high heat until shimmering. Reduce the heat to medium, then carefully add the bean sticks in batches. Fry for 30 seconds or until golden – they will curl but that's fine. Remove with a slotted spoon and drain on paper towel. Serve with the coconut bean sprout salad and rice. ◑

Red lentil kifta

1 cup (200 g) split red lentils
(see Ingredients)

1 clove garlic, crushed

½ onion, finely diced

½ cup (80 g) cracked bulgar wheat

handful of mint leaves,
roughly chopped

handful of flat-leaf parsley leaves,
roughly chopped

1 teaspoon dried oregano

1 tablespoon sumac

1 tablespoon Turkish red pepper
paste (biber salcasi)

1 teaspoon cumin seeds, toasted

1 tablespoon tomato paste (puree)

1 tablespoon extra virgin olive oil

1 tablespoon salt flakes

½ teaspoon cracked black pepper

1 head baby red cos

1 head baby green cos

½ cup (140 g) natural yoghurt

This is a brilliant 'can't be bothered' dinner at the end of a hot summer's day. It screams freshness, has got plenty going on nutritionally and, as bulgar is a wholegrain, is also deceptively filling. Kifta also make a great little pass-around welcome to keep guests happy while you are whipping up the main event in the kitchen. In fact, this is a perfect precedent to the Fig and caramelised onion pizza with rocket on page 74.

I always look for tight, robust-leafed baby cos. The leaves should have some substance and weight so if they are a little sad, nip a cut on the base of the lettuce and pop it into tepid water. Osmosis will take care of the rest. Don't get too hung up on the chilli paste. I use Turkish red pepper paste, which is traditionally made with sun-dried chilli peppers, but it's fine to use any paste with a similar heat and texture.

1 Place the lentils, garlic and onion in a saucepan and cover with 3 cups (750 ml) of water. Bring to a simmer over medium heat and cook for 15 minutes or until the lentils are tender. Remove from the heat, then stir in the bulgar wheat, pop a lid on top and leave to stand for 20 minutes. Remove the lid and transfer the lentil mixture to a large bowl. Leave to cool at room temperature for 10 minutes or so.

2 When the lentil mixture is cool, add the mint, parsley, oregano, sumac, red pepper paste, cumin seeds, tomato paste, olive oil, salt and pepper. Stir until well combined. Form the mixture into golfball-sized balls, then roll them into 5 cm torpedoes.

3 To serve, separate the cos leaves and lay them on a platter. Arrange the kifta on top and drizzle with yoghurt. ◗

(Not) baked beans
WITH baked eggs

1¼ cups (250 g) dried kabuli chickpeas (see Ingredients), soaked overnight in cold water

2 tablespoons extra virgin olive oil

1 small onion, chopped

2 cloves garlic, crushed

600 g really ripe tomatoes, chopped

2 tablespoons maple syrup

2 tablespoons dijon mustard

1 bay leaf

1½ teaspoons salt flakes

¼ teaspoon cracked black pepper

6 large free-range eggs

toasted sourdough, to serve

One of my favourite breakfasts, this dish is a nutritional powerhouse. The recipe took a while for me to perfect: I tried baking chickpeas the way I would Boston baked beans, but it always resulted in an epic failure that left me scratching my head. The chickpeas came out crunchy every time, no matter what I did. First I tried soaking them for longer than usual. Then I tried adding some acid (vinegar or lemon juice) to the soaking water, a surefire way to get a creamy chickpea – but nothing worked.

Then I remembered that while soaking in an acidic solution softens chickpeas, cooking in the same solution has the opposite effect. That was it: while the chickpeas were simmering, the natural acids in the tomato were toughening them up, making the skins crunchy. Mystery solved! So, for this reason, unlike in a traditional baked bean recipe, the chickpeas are cooked separately to the tomato sauce. The only problem I have now is what to call the recipe . . .

1 Drain the chickpeas and rinse them well, discarding the soaking water. Place them and 3 cups (750 ml) of cold water in a saucepan over medium heat and bring to a rapid simmer for 45 minutes, until the chickpeas are tender and nestled in just a small amount of water. Remove from the heat and set aside.

2 Place a large heavy-based frying pan over medium heat. Add the olive oil and onion and saute until translucent. Add the garlic and continue to saute, then add the tomato (including any juices), maple syrup, mustard, bay leaf, salt and pepper. Turn the heat to low and simmer for about 40 minutes, stirring occasionally, until the sauce is rich. Fold in the chickpeas.

3 Preheat the oven to 180°C fan-forced (200°C conventional). Divide the chickpeas among six 1 cup (250 ml) ramekins and crack an egg on top of each. Place the ramekins on a baking tray and bake for 13 minutes or until the whites are set but the yolks are still runny (5 minutes longer if you like harder yolks).

4 Serve the baked chickpeas and eggs with toasted sourdough. ◑

Serves 4

Blue corn chips
<u>WITH</u> refried beans,
avocado salsa <u>AND</u> corn

2 corn cobs, in their husks

2 avocados, flesh roughly chopped

1 large green chilli, seeded
and sliced

juice of 1 lime

½ red onion, sliced

⅓ cup (80 ml) extra virgin olive oil

salt flakes and cracked
black pepper

200 g blue corn chips

½ cup (60 g) grated cheddar

large handful of coriander leaves

Refried beans

1 cup (200 g) dried kidney beans,
soaked overnight in cold water

100 ml extra virgin olive oil

½ red onion, diced

2 cloves garlic, chopped

½ teaspoon dried serrano chillies
(or any hot dried chilli)

2 teaspoons cumin seeds

1 teaspoon salt flakes

Navigating your way around diet fads can be a little overwhelming. I'm too old to care anymore but I do have a simple rule. If it is old food – if past civilisations used it as a staple – then I reckon it's probably okay. I figure the success of a society's survival depended on sound nutritional practice, so through years of trial and error, they pretty much worked out what was best to grow and eat. (I believe in science but it often just confirms that what we used to eat was actually right; we just got a little off track in the last century or so.) Blue corn is a good example. An indigenous American staple for centuries, it has a far superior nutritional profile than common corn and, importantly for non-meat eaters, it is also a more complete plant protein than white or yellow corn.

You can grab some black beans for this recipe, but I prefer kidney beans for their colour. Traditionally the beans are simmered with the Mexican herb epazote, but this is not easy to find locally and the beans are fine without it. While epazote does impart flavour, it mostly acts to aid digestion (like the use of asafetida in Indian cooking). Anyway, the real action happens in the pan afterwards, when the beans are fried and mushed with chilli to create an amazing creamy texture and taste.

1 For the refried beans, drain the kidney beans and transfer them to a large saucepan with 1.5 litres of water. Bring to a simmer over low heat and cook for 1–1½ hours until tender. Drain, reserving the cooking water.

2 Heat the olive oil in a large heavy-based frying pan over low heat. Add the onion, garlic, chilli and cumin, and fry for 5 minutes or until soft. Add the beans and salt and cook for a few minutes, then mash with a spud masher, gradually adding the reserved cooking liquid as needed to prevent burning and sticking. Continue to fry the mashed beans gently for 30 minutes, stirring often.

3 Meanwhile, place the corn cobs in a large bowl and cover with boiling water. Soak for 5 minutes, then drain. Heat a chargrill pan over high heat and chargrill the corn for 20 minutes, turning often; the husks will burn but don't worry! Remove from the heat and allow to cool slightly, then discard the husks and cut the corn kernels off the cob.

4 Place the avocado, chilli, lime juice, onion and olive oil in a bowl, then season with salt and pepper and gently mix until combined.

5 Preheat the grill to medium–high. Divide the corn chips among heatproof plates or pans, add the beans and sprinkle with cheese. Grill for 5 minutes or until the cheese is melted and golden. To serve, top with corn, avocado salsa and coriander. ◗

Passionfruit AND coconut water jelly

1 level teaspoon agar agar

2 cups (500 ml) coconut water

80 g caster sugar

200 g passionfruit (about 10 large),
cut in half, pulp scooped out

80 g coconut palm sugar
(see page 70)

280 ml coconut cream

pinch of salt flakes

2 kaffir lime leaves, finely sliced

6 Vietnamese mint leaves

Syrup

2 teaspoons basil seeds

2 tablespoons coconut water

80 g coconut palm sugar

Jelly is always a little other-worldly, somehow a bit wrong and fun: after all, food shouldn't really move. Agar jelly is quick, simple and vegan friendly, as it is derived from the gelatinous substance in kelp. Like gelatine, agar needs to be brought to a simmer. The difference is that agar will just keep on setting more and more over time until it turns into a super-ball or eventually cracks. From a cook's perspective, if you use too much gelatine you can always whip the jelly out of the fridge for 20 mins or so to soften it, but you don't have this luxury with agar. It is solid at room temp so I use a very low ratio of agar to liquid and always eat the jellies fairly promptly. The basil seeds have a fantastic gooeyness, like the gummy stuff inside okra, with a little crunch in the centre. Buy them at Asian grocers, or just accompany the jellies with a simple palm sugar syrup.

Coconut water is easy to extract yourself. Grab a fresh young coconut and shake it to ensure that it sloshes. Give it a stern bash with the back of a knife around the circumference and the shell will yield. Prize it apart with your hands to split the inner flesh and hold over a bowl to collect the perfumed, slightly soapy water.

1 Whisk the agar and coconut water in a small saucepan. Bring to a simmer over medium–low heat and cook for 5 minutes, stirring continuously. Remove from the heat and pour half the mixture into another small saucepan. Add the caster sugar to one of the pans and stir to combine. Return to the heat and cook for 1–2 minutes, stirring, until the sugar dissolves. Remove from the heat and whisk in the passionfruit pulp. Spoon the mixture into six ¼ cup (60 ml) moulds, about 1 tablespoon per mould. Place in the fridge for 5–10 minutes to semi-set, then give it a slight tip – the mixture needs to be at least the consistency of thick cream. If it isn't, give it another 10 minutes, but don't let it get 'pencil eraser hard' or the next layer will not adhere.

2 Meanwhile, add the palm sugar, coconut cream and salt to the agar and coconut water in the other saucepan and stir to combine. Place over medium–low heat and cook for 3–5 minutes, stirring, until the sugar dissolves. Be careful not to overcook, otherwise the coconut cream will split. Remove from the heat and leave to cool to about 40°C (around body temperature). Carefully pour this mixture over the passionfruit layer. You don't need to return the jellies to the fridge – they will be ready in 30 minutes at room temperature. Just make sure they are served within 3 hours as they set really hard.

3 To make the syrup, soak the basil seeds in the coconut water for 10 minutes. Place the palm sugar and ⅓ cup (80 ml) of water in a small saucepan over low heat and heat until the sugar dissolves. Set aside to cool for 5 minutes, then stir in the coconut water and soaked basil seeds. Dip the moulds in warm water and carefully turn out the jellies onto plates. Garnish with kaffir lime and mint and drizzle over the syrup. ●

Chocolate, cherry AND coconut bars

⅓ cup (80 ml) verjuice

300 g dried cherries

½ cup (125 ml) runny honey

⅓ cup (80 g) virgin coconut oil

300 g shredded coconut

200 g dark chocolate
(70 per cent cocoa), finely chopped

Commercially produced versions of this chocolatey treat often contain a bunch of nasty numbers among the numerous ingredients, as well as gelatine. Fair enough, our demand for food with a long shelf-life on tap 24/7 may push manufacturers to commit all sorts of food crimes, but I say just make your own. Dark chocolate, cherry and coconut is a classic flavour combination and you will find yourself very popular around grown-ups who are still little kids inside.

For me, big, fat juicy cherries are synonymous with Christmas Day. However, once the festive rush is over some industrious growers get busy and the first farmers' markets of the year offer some ridiculous indulgences. Cherry juice is an unmissable luxury and I always grab a couple of bottles, but if I see maraschino or glace cherries I generally back away very slowly from the vendor – they just scare me. During processing, the water content is replaced with sugar syrup and I feel it's a culpable offence to subject the most magnificent of all stone fruits to sugar hell.

Dried cherries are a different ballgame, however. None of the tartness of the sourer varieties is lost, the tannins get pushed to a new realm and the residual sugars take on a complex caramel flavour, plus the texture becomes pleasantly chewy. If you fancy it, you can also make your own dried cherries by pitting 600 g of fresh cherries and baking them in a 170°C oven for 30–40 minutes or until they've lost 50 per cent of their moisture. In this recipe the dried cherries are then plumped up in verjuice, which just adds to the intensity.

1 Bring the verjuice to a simmer in a small saucepan over medium heat. Remove from the heat and add the dried cherries. Cover and leave for 10–15 minutes to plump up. Stir in the honey and coconut oil, then return the pan to low heat and warm gently, stirring until smooth.

2 Line a 25 cm × 20 cm baking tray with baking paper. Transfer the cherry mixture to a food processor, add the coconut and blitz until it comes together in a ball. Transfer the mixture to the prepared tray, pressing firmly to ensure it binds. Place in the freezer for 1–2 hours. When firm, remove from the freezer and cut into 12 bars, about 10 cm × 4 cm.

3 To melt the chocolate, bring a saucepan of water to the boil, then remove from the heat and set a heatproof bowl on top. Place the chocolate in the bowl and leave to stand, stirring occasionally, until melted. Brush the melted chocolate over the top of the bars, coating them evenly.

4 Store the bars in an airtight container in the fridge for up to a month. ◗

AUT

Celeriac AND pear soup

750 g celeriac, peeled

2 pears, skin on,
quartered and cored

1 tablespoon lemon juice

110 ml extra virgin olive oil

salt flakes and cracked
black pepper

1 large onion, diced

1 tablespoon lemon thyme leaves,
finely chopped

4 cloves garlic, crushed

250 g starchy potatoes (such as
colibans, kennebecs or russets),
peeled and chopped into
2 cm cubes

3 cups (750 ml) milk

1 teaspoon finely grated lemon zest

1½ tablespoons vincotto

chervil sprigs, to garnish

It's a classic duo, celeriac and pear. Celeriac is sweeter and earthier than celery with a much gentler aniseed flavour, so the chervil garnish helps bring this out. For the pears, I'd suggest a crispy nashi or beurre bosc for texture. It doesn't matter that much for the soup, but you definitely want the matchsticks to be crisp.

Vincotto is just poor people's sugar, really. Boiled-down grape must was being used as a condiment long before the British got busy colonising and wealthy Victorians started filling their fancy silver pots with the white stuff. Nowadays though, vincotto is sort of fancy and cheffy. Here it adds a lovely, musty port-like sweetness to the soup.

1 Cut about 70 g of the celeriac and a quarter of the pear into matchsticks. Place in a bowl and splash with lemon juice, then set aside at room temperature.

2 Preheat the oven to 200°C fan-forced (220°C conventional). Chop the remaining celeriac into 2 cm cubes and place on a baking tray with the remaining pear quarters. Drizzle with 2 tablespoons of olive oil and season generously with salt and pepper. Roast for 30 minutes or until the celeriac and pear are soft and coloured.

3 Heat 2 tablespoons of olive oil in a heavy-based saucepan over low heat. Add the onion and lemon thyme and saute for 4–5 minutes or until the onion is glassy, then add the garlic and saute for 2 minutes or until softened. Add the potato, milk and lemon zest and bring to a simmer. Fold in the roasted celeriac and pear, then pour in 700 ml of water and simmer for about 15 minutes or until the potato is soft. Remove from the heat and puree with a stick blender. If the soup is too thick, add a touch more water. Adjust the seasoning.

4 Bowl up and drizzle with vincotto and the remaining olive oil. Sprinkle with the pear and celeriac matchsticks and garnish with chervil sprigs. ◗

Pearl barley WITH pomegranate, rocket AND walnuts

60 g butter

4 golden shallots, finely diced

4 cloves garlic, crushed

1 tablespoon thyme leaves, chopped

1½ cups (300 g) pearl barley, soaked for at least 1 hour, overnight if possible

¼ cup (60 ml) verjuice

1 bay leaf

1.1 litres water

salt flakes and cracked black pepper

big handful of rocket

⅓ cup (80 ml) extra virgin olive oil

handful of walnuts

2 pomegranates, seeds only

¼ cup (60 ml) pomegranate molasses

¼ preserved lemon, pith discarded, finely sliced

Pomegranate is one of those garden miracles. A little flower pops out on a branch sometime in late spring. A teeny fruit begins to grow behind the flower throughout summer and the anticipation is almost too much to bear as it starts to redden. Come autumn there appears a weird, slightly weather-beaten fruit wearing a funny crown that crunches when you squeeze it. Then, after five or six months of waiting, you finally pick the fruit. You cut through the flesh and it's filled with sticky red juice and a mountain of jewels. Finally, you taste it and the seeds pop in your mouth, releasing sweet, sour and tannic flavour explosions. And people say fruit is boring!

In this recipe, I love the pomegranate's outrageous flavours combined with the (by comparison) rather staid and sensible pearl barley. It's a dish of extremes and a completely fulfilling meal on a chilly night.

1 Place a large heavy-based saute or frying pan over medium heat. Add the butter and leave it to melt then bubble and froth, until it browns slightly. Add the shallot and saute for 4 minutes until soft and glassy, then add the garlic and thyme and saute until the garlic becomes highly aromatic and a little coloured.

2 Drain the pearl barley and add it to the pan. Toast the grains for about 5 minutes, stirring frequently to prevent burning. Deglaze the pan with the verjuice, then add the bay leaf and a ladleful of water and cook, stirring constantly, until the liquid has been absorbed. Continue in this way until all the water has been used and the pearl barley is tender, about 20–25 minutes. Season with salt and pepper.

3 Blend together the rocket, olive oil and a pinch of salt in a food processor.

4 Toast the walnuts in a dry frying pan over low heat for 5 minutes, tossing regularly to prevent burning.

5 To serve, divide the pearl barley among plates. Muddle up the pomegranate seeds in the pomegranate molasses and spoon alongside. Drizzle with the rocket oil and garnish with preserved lemon and toasted walnuts. ◑

Pumpkin, lupin <u>AND</u> sandalwood muffins

600 g (½ small) butternut pumpkin (squash)

1 tablespoon extra virgin olive oil

⅔ cup (130 g) rice flour

½ cup (60 g) lupin flour

½ cup (75 g) potato flour

½ teaspoon ground cinnamon

½ teaspoon ground nutmeg

¼ teaspoon ground cloves

½ teaspoon baking powder

1 teaspoon bicarbonate of soda

1 teaspoon salt flakes

½ cup (180 g) robust honey (such as mallee or blue gum)

¼ cup (60 ml) milk

2 free-range eggs, lightly beaten

½ cup (125 ml) melted butter

¼ cup (30 g) raw sandalwood nuts (or macadamias), roughly chopped

Lupin has been traditionally and unfairly regarded as the poorer cousin of the lentil: a legume without any real social status. A great nitrogen-fixer and soil improver, it also tolerates poor-quality soils, which is all good and well for the land but probably doesn't help its reputation as a not-sexy food. However, the humble, sweet and nutty lupin may be about to have its moment, as people cotton on to its impressive protein content and antioxidant and prebiotic values. It's also a great gluten-free option. When baking with it, you'll just need to lighten up the dough with plenty of raising agent (bi carb and baking powder).

Sandalwood is probably best known for its fragrant oil, but the nuts have an absolutely unique flavour: creamy but not oily or waxy – quite unusual. They've become quite a hit in restaurants lately and the quality of sandalwood nuts being produced by a growing Western Australian industry is impressive. I recommend you go online, seek some out and give them a shot. In this recipe, they work perfectly with the sweetness of the pumpkin. There really is nothing quite like them, but you can always use macadamias instead.

1 To make a pumpkin puree, preheat the oven to 180°C fan-forced (200°C conventional) and lightly oil a roasting tin. Carve the pumpkin into big wedges and toss in olive oil. Roast for 1 hour until very soft. Leave to cool a little, then peel off the skin and process the flesh to a very smooth paste. You should end up with about 1¼ cups (320 g) of mashed pumpkin. Keep the oven on.

2 Place the flours, spices, baking powder, bicarb soda and salt in a large bowl and stir until well combined. Add the honey, milk, eggs, melted butter, pumpkin puree and nuts, stirring until well combined.

3 Line a large 8-hole muffin tin with well-greased muffin cases and fill with the batter until three-quarters full. Bake the muffins for 30 minutes or until a skewer inserted into the centre comes out clean. These are delicious served warm with butter. ◖

1 bunch baby carrots, trimmed
and halved if large

1 bunch baby beets, trimmed
and halved or quartered if large

3 celery sticks, cut into batons

1 cup (about 150 g) pickles –
onions, cornichons, whatever
you have

half a loaf of really good sourdough

extra virgin olive oil, to serve

salt flakes

Bagna cauda

150 ml milk

15 cloves garlic, peeled

100 ml extra virgin olive oil

70 ml verjuice

1 tablespoon red wine vinegar

1 large red chilli, seeded
and finely sliced

10 salted capers, salt gently
rubbed off, roughly chopped

1 teaspoon salt flakes

cracked black pepper

Parmesan mayonnaise

3 free-range eggs

¼ cup (60 ml) verjuice

1 tablespoon dijon mustard

200 ml extra virgin olive oil

30 g parmesan, grated

1 tablespoon boiling water

cracked black pepper

Baby root veg WITH parmesan mayo AND bagna cauda

This is all about new-season extra virgin olive oil and autumn's really good baby root veg. It's a dish of stunning simplicity, a couple of fancy-but-easy sauces anda riot of colour on a massive platter. There are no rules about which new-season oil you should like, but when you're sampling the options a teeny square of bread and a piddley puddle of oil just doesn't cut it in my opinion. My way is to grab at least 10 ml in a shot glass; I have a sniff, gob it and suck some air for a few seconds, then swirl it around my mouth like a wine wally for another few seconds before swallowing. The grass and fruit in the oil is the sensation on the palate; the pepper is the tickling down the back of your throat; and the butteriness is how long it hangs about for. I like it to stay for about 10–12 seconds. Longer than this suggests a 'fat' oil that can become cloying.

Above all though, if someone starts banging on to you about freshly mown grass or bananas and why you *should* like their oil, ignore them and just go with what you like – simple. Oh, and if it's a first press don't be scared of cloudiness or sediment at the bottom: that's part of the deal.

1 Place the carrots, beets, celery, pickles and bread on a serving platter with dipping bowls ready for the sauces.

2 For the bagna cauda, place the milk and garlic in a small saucepan over low heat for 10–15 minutes or until the garlic has softened. Discard the milk and rinse the garlic in a little water. Place the olive oil in a clean saucepan, add the garlic and gently heat until it starts to colour and smell nutty.

3 Place the verjuice, vinegar and chilli in a small saucepan over medium heat and cook for a minute or so until reduced by half. Remove from the heat and add the garlic and olive oil, then add the capers and salt. Season with pepper and muddle with a fork to break down the garlic. Spoon the bagna cauda into a dipping bowl.

4 For the parmesan mayonnaise, place the unpeeled eggs in a small saucepan of water and bring to a simmer over high heat. Once simmering, turn down the heat and cook for 2 minutes. Plunge the eggs into iced water to cool, then peel. Place in a food processor with the verjuice and mustard and pulse until smooth and well combined. Slowly drizzle in the olive oil, then add the parmesan. Finally, add the boiling water. Season with pepper, then spoon the mayo into a dipping bowl.

5 To serve, place the extra virgin olive oil and salt flakes on the table with the veg, pickles, bread and sauces, and invite everyone to help themselves. ◗

Mock duck ball soup

I'm not a fan of those faux meats, which are often gluten-set in all sorts of weird meat-like shapes and colours. I've called this 'mock duck' because of the stringiness of the mushrooms and carrots. There is a time and place for beautiful, silky softness, but according to many vegetarian menus this is the only texture available. I'm just saying it's good to get some stuff stuck between your teeth now and again.

I've used tamari and potato or tapioca flour here because I am trying to look out for the gluten-challenged. Substitute soy and cornflour if gluten isn't an issue for you. And, as with most of my recipes, feel free to ditch the egg if you are from planet vegan. It isn't a deal-breaker to the overall.

100 g enoki mushrooms, trimmed

cracked white pepper

½ teaspoon sesame oil

Mock duck balls

400 g firm tofu

3 fresh shiitake mushrooms

½ small carrot, peeled and
cut into matchsticks

2 tablespoons potato flour
r tapioca flour

½ teaspoon salt flakes

pinch of cracked
white pepper

1 free-range egg, beaten

3 spring onions, green parts
finely sliced

2 cups (500 ml) flavour-neutral oil
(see page 33)

Broth

2½ tablespoons flavour-neutral oil

2 spring onions, white parts
very finely chopped

2.5 cm ginger, chopped

4 cloves garlic, chopped

salt flakes

1 cup (120 g) frozen soy beans
(edamame)

2 tablespoons sake

1 litre Shiitake stock (see Basics)

1 tablespoon mirin

2 tablespoons tamari

1 For the mock duck balls, wrap the tofu in a clean tea towel and place on a draining board. Place a 1 kg weight on top and leave for 1 hour to extract any excess liquid.

2 For the broth, heat the oil in a heavy-based frying pan over medium–high heat. Saute the spring onion and ginger until a little colour is knocked onto the ginger, then add the garlic and continue to fry. Add a pinch of salt and the soy beans and fry for another minute or two, then deglaze the pan with the sake. Pour in the shiitake stock and add the mirin, then bring to a simmer over medium heat. Add the tamari, and salt to taste, then remove from the heat and set the broth aside.

3 Remove and discard the stems from the shiitake mushrooms, then slice the caps into fine matchsticks. Place the drained tofu in a food processor and pulse until it resembles fine breadcrumbs. Transfer to a large bowl with the shiitake, carrot, flour, salt, pepper, egg and spring onion, mixing until well combined.

4 Gently heat the oil in a wok over medium heat. Working in batches, shape the tofu mixture into bite-sized balls and drop them into the oil, being careful not to overcrowd the wok. Cook for a minute or two until golden brown, then remove from the wok with a slotted spoon and drain well on paper towel.

5 Place the broth back over medium heat to warm. Divide the mock duck balls among bowls and gently ladle the hot broth over the top. Serve sprinkled with enoki mushrooms, white pepper and sesame oil. ●

Pickled quince AND lentil pies WITH raw beetroot relish

80 g unhulled red lentils
(see Ingredients)

2 tablespoons olive oil

½ large onion, diced

2 cloves garlic, crushed

salt flakes and cracked
black pepper

1 tablespoon plain flour

1 tablespoon tomato paste (puree)

1 bay leaf

1 sprig thyme, leaves picked
and chopped

1 sprig rosemary, leaves picked
and chopped

1 waxy potato (such as kipfler
or bintje), peeled and diced

1 small carrot, peeled and diced

¼ swede, peeled and diced

1½ tablespoons red wine vinegar

445 g sour cream shortcrust
pastry, thawed if frozen,
brought to room temperature

2 tablespoons chopped
flat-leaf parsley

1 free-range egg, lightly beaten

375 g all-butter puff pastry,
thawed if frozen, brought to
room temperature

Pickled quinces

700 ml cider vinegar

300 g sugar

1 tablespoon juniper berries

1 teaspoon black peppercorns

1 bay leaf

3 quinces, peeled, cored
and cut into fat wedges

This is a shameless rip-off of a dish by a couple of legends. Maggie Beer cooked up a lamb and quince pie on an episode of *The Cook and the Chef*, which she named 'Treasure's pickled quince pie'. It turned out this was a nod to one of my old bosses and one of Maggie's close friends and co-workers, food-tech guru Trevor Cook, who is absolutely a treasure in the kitchen! The pickled quinces were amazing, so I just had to swipe the recipe for them. The addition of a raw beet relish provides a nice contrast of freshness to the braised lentils, which are all about chilly days and chillier nights.

1 For the pickled quinces, place all the ingredients except the quinces in a large saucepan over medium heat and stir until the sugar dissolves. Bring to the boil, then add the quinces and simmer for 20 minutes or until they are just tender. Leave to cool, then set 100 g aside to use in the pies. (The remaining pickled quinces will keep in a sterilised jar in the fridge for up to 6 months.)

2 Place the lentils in a saucepan and add 700 ml of water. Bring to the boil over high heat, then reduce the heat to medium–low and simmer for 30 minutes until the lentils are just tender to the bite. Top up the water if the lentils become too dry but keep the liquid level low as you will lose flavour otherwise; you want to end up with lentils nestled in a smidge of water. Set aside.

3 Heat the olive oil in a large heavy-based saucepan over medium–low heat. Add the onion and garlic and stir to combine, then cover and cook for 5 minutes or until the onion is soft and glassy. Increase the heat to medium and cook for a further 4–5 minutes, then season with salt and pepper. Add the flour, tomato paste, bay leaf, thyme, rosemary, potato, carrot and swede, stirring until all the ingredients are combined. Increase the heat to medium–high and deglaze the pan with the vinegar, then add 150 ml of water and reduce the heat to low. Cook for 45 minutes or until the vegetables are tender and sitting in a thick sauce. Remove from the heat and add the lentils, stirring to combine. Leave to cool.

4 Preheat the oven to 180°C fan-forced (200°C conventional).

5 Place the shortcrust pastry on a lightly floured benchtop and roll out to 3 mm. Cut out six 16 cm rounds to line the bottom of six pie tins. Dice the reserved pickled quinces and stir them into the cooled filling mixture along with the parsley. Evenly divide the cool filling among the pastry cases. Brush the edges with the egg.

Pickled quince *and* lentil pies *with* raw beetroot relish *(cont.)*

Raw beetroot relish

2 teaspoons olive oil

1 teaspoon brown mustard seeds

2 tablespoons red wine vinegar

1 tablespoon brown sugar

3 teaspoons salt flakes

cracked black pepper

2 large beetroots,
peeled and grated

6 Roll the puff pastry to a thickness of 2 mm and cut out six 13 cm rounds. Place the lids on top of the pies and press around the edges with a fork to seal. Using a sharp paring knife, trim the pastry and make a tiny hole in the top of each pie to allow steam to escape. Place on a baking tray and bake in the oven for 45 minutes or until the pastry is golden.

7 For the beetroot relish, heat the oil in a frying pan. Add the mustard seeds and fry briefly until they crackle and pop. Add the vinegar, sugar, salt and pepper and bring to the boil. Simmer for 2–3 minutes until the vinegar evaporates slightly, then allow to cool. Add the beetroot and stir well to combine.

8 Serve the pies warm with the beetroot relish. ◗

Serves 6

Mung bean spanakopita

2 tablespoons olive oil

1 onion, diced

1 bunch English spinach,
stems removed

1 cup (100 g) mung bean sprouts

½ bunch spring onions,
white parts finely sliced

½ bunch dill, leaves picked

½ teaspoon grated nutmeg

200 g feta, crumbled

½ cup (85 g) cooked brown rice

2 free-range eggs, lightly beaten

salt flakes and cracked
black pepper

200 g filo pastry

100 g butter, melted

2 teaspoons poppy seeds

I'm usually a 'if it's not broken don't fix it' kind of guy. I respect the classics, and this particular one certainly wasn't broken. I am always left a little hungry after eating spanakopita, however, so one particularly ravenous day I decided to add some leftover brown rice and sprouts to the basic recipe. The rice adds substance, while the mung bean sprouts bring crunch and nuttiness – all worthy embellishments. If you're a vegan, you can lose the egg, no problem, and just substitute some crumbled silken firm tofu for the feta.

1 Preheat the oven to 180°C fan-forced (200°C conventional). Lightly grease a 24 cm × 18 cm baking tin.

2 Heat the olive oil in a large saucepan over low heat. Add the onion, then cover with a lid and cook for 10 minutes until soft. Add the spinach leaves and cook for 3 minutes or until wilted. Drain and leave to cool, then squeeze out any excess moisture.

3 Place the spinach mixture in a large bowl with the sprouts, spring onion, dill, nutmeg, feta, rice and eggs. Season with salt and pepper and mix until well combined.

4 Brush a sheet of filo with melted butter and place in the prepared tin, with the pastry reaching up the sides. Repeat with a further six layers of filo pastry, then spoon the spinach mixture on top. Brush another six filo sheets with butter and place on top of the spinach mixture to seal the filling. Scatter with poppy seeds.

5 Bake for 40–45 minutes or until the pastry is golden brown.

Baked cauliflower fregola WITH hazelnuts AND preserved lemon

1 baby (or fist-sized) cauliflower

300 g fregola

130 g butter

40 g plain flour

2 cups (500 ml) cold milk

70 g grated cheddar

salt flakes and cracked black pepper

pinch of grated nutmeg

120 g stale sourdough breadcrumbs

¼ cup (35 g) hazelnuts, roughly chopped

¼ preserved lemon, rinsed and chopped

small handful of flat-leaf parsley leaves, chopped

8 sprigs thyme, leaves picked

3 free-range eggs, hard-boiled, peeled and chopped

Don't like the smell of cooked cauliflower? Try simmering it lightly and then baking it. The cauli takes on a whole new flavour and may well convert even the most hardened cauliflower-phobe. I really like this dish, especially the way the teeny fregola pebbles (rolled pasta balls) suck up the white sauce. With its toasted breadcrumbs, hard-boiled eggs and chopped parsley, it is essentially a classic polonaise, with just a few liberties taken.

1 Quarter the cauliflower from top to bottom, leaving the maximum amount of stem – on baby caulis it's the best bit. Par-cook it in salted simmering water for about 8 minutes or until just tender. Drain and refresh under cold water, then transfer to a shallow baking tray.

2 Meanwhile, bring a saucepan of salted water to the boil, add the fregola and cook according to the packet instructions (about 10 minutes). Drain, then add the fregola to the cauliflower.

3 Preheat the oven to 200°C fan-forced (220°C conventional). Melt 50 g of butter in a small heavy-based saucepan over low heat. Add the flour and stir for a few minutes to cook but not colour, then slowly add the milk, stirring continuously. Increase the heat to medium and cook, stirring, for about 5 minutes or until the mixture thickens. Stir in the cheddar, then season with salt and pepper and add the nutmeg. Pour the cheese mixture over the cauliflower and fregola, and place in the oven for 5 minutes to heat through.

4 Meanwhile, heat a heavy-based saucepan over medium heat. Add the remaining butter and allow it to fizz and then become aromatic and nut brown, swirling the pan to prevent burning. Add the breadcrumbs and the heat will immediately 'toast' them; quickly tip them into a bowl and season with salt. Add the hazelnuts, preserved lemon and half the parsley and thyme, stirring to combine.

5 Top the baked cauliflower fregola with the breadcrumb mixture and season with pepper. Scatter over the chopped egg and remaining parsley and thyme. ●

Serves 4

Chawan mushi wakame AND shiitake

15 cm dried kombu
(see Ingredients), rinsed

5 dried shiitake mushrooms

¼ cup (60 ml) Japanese soy
sauce or Chinese light soy sauce
(see page 85)

70 ml mirin

salt flakes

4 free-range eggs, lightly beaten

2 tablespoons vegetable oil

pinch of cracked white pepper

100 g enoki mushrooms, trimmed

3 g dried wakame
(see Ingredients), soaked in
warm water for 20 minutes,
or 15 g fresh wakame, chopped

1 spring onion, green part
finely sliced

There is something very satisfying about getting these little silky custards exactly right. They have a super-soft wobbly texture, which I know is not everybody's thing. I think most people are averse to it because food that moves short-circuits our brain – for obvious reasons, I guess, if you're a carnivore. Having been totally horrified by junket as a kid, it took me years to appreciate slippery stuff like this. However, I'm happy to say I have moved on and I am a card-carrying member of the chawan mushi appreciation society. Give these a try and you just might be converted too . . .

1 Place the kombu and shiitake mushrooms in a saucepan with 1 litre of water. Bring to the boil over medium heat, then remove the kombu. Remove the pan from the heat and steep for 10 minutes, then strain, reserving 600 ml of the stock. Set the shiitakes aside. Add the soy sauce, 50 ml of mirin and a pinch of salt and leave to cool to room temperature. When the stock is cool, add the eggs, stirring until well combined, then pass the custard mixture through a fine strainer.

2 Squeeze the reserved shiitake mushrooms dry, then remove the stems and thinly slice the caps. Heat the oil in a small heavy-based frying pan over very high heat and sear the mushrooms quickly but aggressively until coloured. Deglaze the pan with the remaining mirin and season with pepper.

3 Set some of the shiitake and enoki mushrooms aside for garnish, then divide the remaining shiitake and enoki and wakame between four chawans (Japanese soup cups), tea cups or ramekins (120–140 ml capacity). Top with the custard and cover with plastic film.

4 Place a steamer over a saucepan of boiling water. Carefully place the cups in the steamer and cover with a lid. Cook for around 8 minutes (depending on the thickness and size of the cups) or until the custard is just set; it will still be slightly wobbly and a skewer should come out clean. Garnish with the reserved mushrooms and spring onion and eat straight away. ◕

Spelt pasta WITH broccoli, garlic AND almond pesto

grated zest of ½ orange

Spelt pasta

400 g spelt flour

2 free-range eggs

2 free-range egg yolks

Broccoli, garlic and almond pesto

125 g broccoli, roughly chopped

½ cup (125 ml) olive oil

100 g almonds

handful of flat-leaf parsley leaves, roughly chopped

¼ cup (60 ml) lemon juice

2 cloves garlic, peeled

salt flakes and cracked black pepper

½ cup (40 g) grated parmesan

As things get wetter and cooler throughout autumn, our almonds start to come back. Sure, nuts are okay when stored, but the oils are volatile and the best time to eat them is now. Shallow-frying them ramps up the crispness and flavour to a new level. This is also a great dish for not-so-great broccoli – you are just going to blitz most of it anyway. Spelt pasta is lighter and nuttier than its common counterpart. It's also low in gluten and grows well without heaps of fertilisers, so it's a popular organic grain.

1 To make the pasta, combine the flour, eggs and yolks in a food processor by pulsing a few times, then slowly add 120 ml of water and pulse until the dough comes together. Turn out onto the benchtop and knead for 8–10 minutes until smooth and silky. Cover with plastic film and leave to rest for an hour in the fridge.

2 Meanwhile, for the broccoli, garlic and almond pesto, shave off 3 mm broccoli tips to create teeny florets and set them aside. Blanch the rest of the broccoli in a saucepan of salted boiling water for 2–3 minutes or until the stems are tender. Drain well. Heat the olive oil in a small heavy-based frying pan over medium heat and gently fry the almonds until deep brown. Remove with a slotted spoon and spread them out on a tray to cool. Reserve the frying oil and leave to cool.

3 Place the blanched broccoli and the parsley in a food processor with the lemon juice and reserved frying oil. Blend until roughly pureed. Set aside a handful of fried almonds for garnish and add the rest to the food processor, along with the garlic. Continue to blend until the mixture looks like crunchy peanut butter, then season with salt and pepper. Add the parmesan and pulse to blend through. Check the seasoning. (You will have more broccoli pesto than you need for the pasta. Leftovers will keep in a sterilised jar, sealed with olive oil, for up to a fortnight in the fridge.)

4 Divide the pasta dough into three and form into balls. Dust with flour and flatten with the palm of your hand, then roll out to 1 cm thick. Pass through a pasta machine, dusting the rollers and gradually reducing the settings until you reach the thinnest or second-thinnest setting. Lightly flour the benchtop and cut the pasta sheets into 2 cm wide pappardelle with a sharp knife.

5 Cook the pasta in a large saucepan of gently boiling salted water for 2 minutes or until tender to the bite, then drain. Toss through the broccoli pesto while the pasta is still warm. Chop the reserved almonds and sprinkle them over the top, along with the orange zest and a scattering of broccoli tips. ●

Sort of mulligatawny lentils

2 tablespoons vegetable oil

1 onion, chopped

12 fresh curry leaves

2 cloves garlic, chopped

1 tablespoon finely chopped ginger

1 teaspoon ground cumin

1 teaspoon ground coriander

2 teaspoons madras curry powder

½ teaspoon ground turmeric

¼ teaspoon cayenne pepper

2 potatoes, peeled and diced

2 carrots, peeled and sliced

2 celery sticks, chopped

1 cup (220 g) French-style green lentils (see Ingredients)

¼ cup (60 ml) lime juice

salt flakes and cracked black pepper

natural yoghurt, to serve

coriander leaves, to garnish

lime wedges, to serve

pappadams, to serve

Most Anglo–Indian dishes, like mulligatawny, carry a fair wad of British tradition. This means they often contain lots of meat, with the meat then often obliterated during cooking. (I can say that about the Brits because I'm one of them.) Fortunately, with this soup, the British couldn't resist the lure of India's deft and wonderful spice-blending. In my opinion, it's this, combined with a squeeze of lemon and a dollop of yoghurt, that makes the dish a winner. The meat is definitely not missed here.

1 Heat the oil in a large heavy-based saucepan over medium–low heat. Add the onion and curry leaves and saute for a few minutes, then add the garlic, ginger, cumin, ground coriander, curry powder, turmeric and cayenne, and stir until well combined. Cover with a lid and cook for 10 minutes or until the onion is soft and glassy.

2 Add 2 litres of water to the saucepan, along with the potato, carrot, celery and lentils. Bring to the boil, then reduce the heat and simmer for 45 minutes or until the vegetables and lentils are tender.

3 Using a stick blender, puree the soup until smooth – or if you want a more rustic finish, leave as is. Add the lime juice and season generously with salt and pepper. If the soup is too thick, add a little water.

4 Ladle the soup into bowls and top with yoghurt and coriander leaves. Serve with lime wedges and pappadams. ◑

Serves 6

Mushroom terrine

200 g portobello mushrooms

150 g king brown mushrooms

150 g fresh shiitake mushrooms

20 g dried porcini, soaked
in warm water for 20 minutes

1 tablespoon olive oil

salt flakes

200 g enoki mushrooms, trimmed

150 g oyster mushrooms, torn

2 cloves garlic, skin on, bruised

2 golden shallots, chopped,
skins reserved

small handful of flat-leaf parsley,
chopped, stalks reserved

1 sprig thyme, plus 1 tablespoon
chopped thyme, extra

½ teaspoon black peppercorns

1 bay leaf

8 g agar agar

1 teaspoon chopped marjoram

2 tablespoons green peppercorns,
roughly chopped

extra virgin olive oil or mayonnaise,
to serve

chives, to garnish

thin toast, to serve

The mention of terrines usually sends people into conniptions but a little knowledge is power. Firstly, you should know that a really fresh mushroom does not feel like a brand-new kitchen sponge (i.e. lighter than a helium balloon). Fresh mushrooms that are grown and stored well will have a certain weight to them due to moisture content, so shop where the food chain is short and the growers are good. Mushrooms from a market are better. Having said that, this dish relies on an agar solution to hold everything together and even if the mushrooms are not the very freshest, they will take as much liquid as they need to bind, and the texture and shape of the terrine will be okay regardless. Think of that new kitchen sponge sitting in a shallow puddle of water: it will end up the same as a wet one sitting in the puddle . . . eventually.

Agar agar is a natural setting agent derived from seaweed and it is easy to use. Here you just whisk it into the warm mushroom stock and bring to a simmer. Once it reaches this temperature, it swells and will start to gel as it cools. Unlike animal-derived gelatine, it sets rapidly and holds at room temperature so there is no need to refrigerate it. The important thing in this method is the agar to liquid ratio, which is essential for holding the terrine together. Both the liquid already present in the mushrooms and the soft raw mushrooms distributed throughout the mix will prevent the terrine becoming hard or rubbery. If you do end up with a rock-hard terrine, then either your mushrooms are very old and contained hardly any water or you've left the terrine for too long before eating.

1 Remove the stems from the portobello, king brown and shiitake mushrooms and set them aside. Using a mandolin, finely slice the portobello and king brown caps making them as long and thin as possible. These will be used to line the mould, so it helps to imagine the slices of streaky bacon in a traditional terrine. Set the sliced portobello and king browns aside on a baking tray. Slice the shiitake mushroom caps into matchsticks and set aside in a large bowl.

2 Drain the porcini, reserving the soaking water, then squeeze them dry and chop them into small pieces. Heat the olive oil in a small heavy-based frying pan over high heat and fry the porcini with a pinch of salt until browned. Add to the bowl of shiitake matchsticks, along with the enoki and oyster mushrooms. Set aside.

Mushroom terrine *(cont.)*

3 To make a mushroom stock, place all the reserved mushroom offcuts in a saucepan and add the bruised garlic, shallot skins, parsley stalks, thyme sprig, black peppercorns and bay leaf. Add the soaking water from the porcini and top up with water to make 1.5 litres. Bring to the boil, then reduce the heat to low and simmer for 20 minutes. Remove from the heat and strain the stock into a bowl, squashing the mushrooms with the back of a ladle to extract all the liquid. Return the strained stock (you should have about 1 litre) to a saucepan and whisk in the agar agar. Bring to a simmer.

4 Pour about 200 ml of the warm stock over the sliced portobellos and king browns on the baking tray. Leave for 5 minutes to absorb, turning the mushrooms over halfway through.

5 Add the chopped shallot, parsley, thyme, marjoram, green peppercorns and 1 tablespoon of salt to the bowl of porcini, shiitakes, enoki and oyster mushrooms. Pour the remaining stock over the top and combine well.

6 Line an 800 ml terrine mould (or long, deep rectangular cake tin) with plastic film, leaving a slight overhang. Place on a baking tray. Line the bottom and the sides of the mould with two-thirds of the portobello and king brown mushrooms. Using a slotted spoon, carefully fill the lined mould with the mushroom and herb mixture. You want the liquid just clinging to the mix but not swimming; there may be a tiny bit of liquid remaining, depending on how much your mushrooms have absorbed. Top with the remaining mushroom slices, then cover with the overhanging plastic film. Place another baking tray on top and weigh it down with a couple of tins of food. A bit of excess liquid will ooze out, but don't worry. Leave at room temperature overnight or refrigerate for 4 hours.

7 To help remove the terrine, gently heat the bottom of the mould by submerging it in warm water or placing it over a gas burner. Use a palette knife to ease the terrine away from the sides. Knock it out onto a board and cut the terrine into 1 cm slices with a super-sharp knife (it's best to leave the plastic film on for this and remove it after slicing).

8 Drizzle the terrine with a good olive oil or mayonnaise, garnish with chives and serve with thin crispy toast. ◗

Chestnut souffle

200–250 g chestnuts,
to yield 160 g shelled

90 g butter

¼ cup (35 g) plain flour

200 ml vegetable stock

½ teaspoon thyme leaves, chopped

handful of chopped flat-leaf parsley

finely grated zest of ½ lemon

salt flakes and cracked
black pepper

4 free-range egg yolks

160 g goat's curd

5 free-range egg whites

handful of baby rocket

2 tablespoons vincotto

I remember standing in a bleak, bitumen primary-school yard, violently smashing horse chestnuts on the end of string and not really understanding the aim of the game beyond trying to keep my eyeballs intact when the chestnuts collided. Thankfully this memory has been surpassed by the first time I sampled roast chestnuts. How could I forget slipping the flesh out and tasting that mealy sweetness? Here, chestnuts give great body to an otherwise light and airy soufflé.

If you have an oven that allows top and bottom element heat with no fan, use that setting. This will push heat gently through the bottom of the souffle for rise while the top heat crusts the cap nicely. If not, the fan-setting will do, but I find it inhibits the rise fractionally.

1 Using a sharp knife, cut a small cross on the flat side of each chestnut. Place them in a saucepan, cover with cold water and bring to the boil. Cook for 3 minutes, then drain and refresh under cold water. Peel the skins, making sure you remove both the outside shell and the inside membrane; do this while the chestnuts are still warm or they will become hard to peel. Place the peeled chestnuts in a food processor and pulse to coarse breadcrumbs.

2 Melt the butter in a saucepan over medium heat, then add the chestnuts and flour and cook for a few minutes, stirring. Slowly pour in the stock, then add the thyme, parsley and lemon zest and a scant teaspoon of salt and pepper. Reduce the heat to low and stir until the stock has been absorbed and the mixture is smooth. Remove from the heat and allow to cool to below 60°C, otherwise the eggs will scramble in the next stage. When cool, add the egg yolks one at a time, beating in well with a wooden spoon, then add the goat's curd and mix through.

3 Preheat the oven to 200°C fan-forced (220°C conventional). Grease a 1 litre ovenproof dish and lightly dust with flour. Half-fill a roasting tin with boiling water; you want it to come about 5 cm up the side of the baking dish. Place the roasting tin (but not the dish) in the oven to preheat; the water temp should reach at least 80°C.

4 Place the egg whites and a pinch of salt in a bowl and whisk almost until stiff peaks form but the mixture is not grainy. Place the chestnut mixture in a separate large bowl, add a third of the beaten egg white and fold through. Add the remaining egg white, folding slowly and gently into the chestnut mixture. (I do this with my hands or with a pastry card so as not to knock the air out – this will give you a puffier souffle.) Transfer the mixture to the baking dish and carefully place it in the preheated water bath. Cook for 20 minutes, then reduce the heat to 180°C fan-forced (200°C conventional) and cook for a further 5 minutes until puffed up and well coloured on top.

5 Serve the souffle with a side of rocket drizzled with vincotto. ◑

Chocolate caponata with white polenta AND fried celery leaves

1 tablespoon pine nuts, toasted

2 tablespoons caperberries, halved

large handful of basil leaves

large handful of chopped flat-leaf parsley

cracked black pepper

Caponata

2 large eggplants (aubergines), cut into 3 cm cubes

¾ cup (180 ml) olive oil

salt flakes

½ bunch celery, chopped, inner white leaves reserved

1 large onion, diced

3 cloves garlic, crushed

1 tablespoon dark brown sugar

2 grosse lisse tomatoes (or any big old ugly ripe tomatoes!), chopped

85 ml aged sweet vinegar

1 tablespoon salted capers, gently rubbed to remove salt

¾ cup (120 g) pitted kalamata olives

30 g couverture dark chocolate (70 per cent cocoa), roughly chopped

Polenta

2 cups (500 ml) milk

1½ cups (250 g) fine white polenta

salt flakes and cracked black pepper

100 g gruyere (or whatever cheese you like – parmesan, romano, etc)

60 g butter, chopped

It's a 'grows together, goes together' dish for early autumn. Eggplants and big, old ripe tomatoes are finishing up, while celery is at its cheap best and the tender inner leaves make a great crispy garnish when fried. Chocolate, a traditional addition in some regional variations of this classic dish, gives the caponata a deep complexity.

I never wash capers. This relatively new industry to Australia is water-wise, sustainable and thriving thanks to our excess sunshine, and produces some absolutely stunning examples. I find they just need a rub with a tea towel to knock any excess salt off. I may be wrong, but I feel that rinsing these brilliantly grown local buds is just washing flavour and texture down the drain.

1 Preheat the oven to 180°C fan-forced (200°C conventional). For the caponata, place the eggplant in a baking dish with ¼ cup (60 ml) of olive oil and a little salt, tossing until well coated. Roast for 20 minutes or until tender. Set aside.

2 Meanwhile, for the polenta, combine the milk and 1 cup (250 ml) of water in a large saucepan over medium heat, and heat until just below boiling point. Reduce the heat to low and slowly add the polenta, stirring continuously. Season with salt and pepper. Continue stirring to prevent sticking, adding extra liquid if required. When the polenta is soft, add the cheese and butter and stir until melted and well combined. Remove from the heat and pop a lid on top to keep the polenta warm.

3 Heat ¼ cup (60 ml) of olive oil in a large saucepan over medium heat. Add the inner white celery leaves and fry for 2 minutes or until crispy. Remove from the pan with a slotted spoon and leave to drain on paper towel.

4 Add the onion and garlic to the same saucepan and saute for 4–5 minutes or until glassy. Add the chopped celery and cook for 1–2 minutes, then add the sugar, tomato and 2½ teaspoons of salt and cook for 10 minutes or until soft. Add the vinegar and reduce for about 3–5 minutes until sticky. Add the roasted eggplant, capers, olives and remaining olive oil, then fold in the chocolate until it melts. Check the seasoning.

5 To serve, spoon the polenta onto plates and top with the caponata and fried celery leaves. Scatter over the pine nuts, caperberries, basil, parsley and a little pepper. ◗

Chargrilled leeks <u>WITH</u> polenta, gorgonzola <u>AND</u> herb oil

1 cup (170 g) coarse polenta

salt flakes and cracked
black pepper

½ cup (60 g) pitted green olives

⅓ cup (80 ml) olive oil

24 pencil leeks, trimmed
and washed well

50 g gorgonzola dolce

Herb oil

½ bunch flat-leaf parsley,
leaves picked

¼ bunch chives, leaves picked

¼ bunch tarragon, leaves picked

¼ bunch chervil, leaves picked

¼ cup (60 ml) olive oil

salt flakes

You'll see pencil-sized leeks in early to mid autumn and they are perfect for this recipe. Just remember if they're bigger than fat spring onions, they're 'teenage' leeks rather than babies, and you'll need to blanch them for 2–3 minutes prior to chargrilling. I leave the little roots hanging off because when immature they are palatable and crisp up nicely while the rest of the leek stem softens on the grill.

The coarse polenta is also chargrilled and the resulting dish is smoky and robust, countered by the sweet (dolce) gorgonzola with its funky overtones. It is accompanied by the delicate herbs, a highly aromatic medley that is whizzed up and immersed in oil to carry the subtle flavours.

1 In a saucepan over medium heat, bring 2 cups (500 ml) of water to the boil. Slowly rain in the polenta, whisking continuously, then turn down the heat to very low. Season with salt and cook the polenta gently for about 20 minutes until thick, stirring occasionally. Pour the polenta into a 15 cm square container and place in the fridge to set for at least an hour.

2 For the herb oil, very finely chop all the herbs or pulse them in a food processor, then combine with the olive oil and a pinch of salt.

3 Heat a chargrill pan over medium heat. Rip up or cut the polenta into 3–4 cm chunks. Lightly coat the polenta and olives with a couple of tablespoons of olive oil. Place them in the pan and grill on both sides until charred and a little smoky. Set aside.

4 Toss the leeks in the remaining olive oil and season with salt and pepper. Working in batches, chargrill the leeks in the same pan for 5–7 minutes, turning occasionally, until well past golden and cooked completely. Don't worry if the wispy roots are a little blackened.

5 Arrange the leeks, polenta and olives on plates and crumble over the gorgonzola. Drizzle with the herb oil and serve. ◗

Serves 4

Water spinach WITH honey, soy AND black sesame tofu

500 g firm tofu

2 tablespoons light soy sauce

2 teaspoons dark soy sauce

1 tablespoon robust honey
(such as mallee or blue gum)

⅓ cup (80 ml) vegetable oil

1 tablespoon granulated garlic

2 cm ginger, peeled and
cut into matchsticks

2 bunches water spinach,
stems cut into 4 cm lengths and
leaves sliced in half

1 tablespoon cornflour mixed with
2 tablespoons cold water

1 tablespoon black sesame seeds

1 large red chilli, finely sliced
(seeds and all)

1 spring onion, finely sliced

steamed jasmine rice, to serve

Honey and soy may be an cliched duo, but if you use a robust (i.e. not viscous and candy-sweet) honey and bitter black sesame seeds, you'll enjoy a grown-up combination that isn't just for kids. You'll find water spinach (sometimes known as swamp spinach or kangkong) easily enough at Asian grocers. It is mild and almost sweet in flavour, so if you need to substitute, very young baby spinach will do (at a pinch). And before you scream at me for using granulated garlic, can I just say in my defense that it delivers a uniquely sticky texture and nutty flavour when taken to the edge of cooking – a method I wouldn't use with fresh garlic as it would just burn and turn bitter. Be a little daring and try it.

1 Wrap the tofu in a tea towel. Place on a draining board and press with a 1 kg weight to extract any excess liquid. Leave to drain for 1 hour.

2 Rip the tofu into bite-sized chunks, then place in a shallow bowl with the soy sauces and honey and turn to coat. Leave to marinate for 30 minutes.

3 Heat a wok over high heat. Add the oil and, when shimmering, add the garlic and fry for about 5–10 seconds until nutty and pale brown; be careful not to let it burn. Add the ginger and marinated tofu. Allow the tofu to stick a little bit to the wok and colour up in places, then add the remaining marinade and water spinach stems. Continue to stir-fry for a minute or so, then add the cornflour mixture and stir to thicken. Finally, add the spinach leaves and allow to wilt. Sprinkle with sesame seeds and remove the wok from the heat.

4 Garnish with chilli and spring onion and serve with steamed rice. ◑

Shabu shabu

9–10 cm dried kombu
(see Ingredients)

2 carrots, peeled and thinly sliced

¼ Chinese cabbage, shredded

200 g firm tofu, cut into
bite-sized pieces

1 bunch bok choy, trimmed

8 spring onions, cut into batons

2 large field mushrooms, sliced

50 g fresh shiitake mushrooms,
sliced

100 g enoki mushrooms, trimmed

50 g shimeji mushrooms, trimmed

50 g oyster mushrooms,
ripped if large

3½ cups (875 ml) Shiitake stock
(see Basics)

steamed jasmine rice, to serve

Dipping sauce

½ cup (75 g) white sesame seeds

¼ cup (60 ml) mirin

1 tablespoon white sugar

1 tablespoon rice vinegar

¼ cup (60 ml) light soy sauce

½ teaspoon grated garlic

½ cup (125 ml) Shiitake stock
(see above)

I like to work for my food sometimes and this dish is absolutely fantastic. It's probably incorrect to call the recipe 'shabu shabu' if it doesn't involve razor-thin strips of beef being 'swished swished' in the soup with chopsticks, but the essence of the dish is still here.

If you don't have a steamboat you can get by, but I love the fire popping out of the chimney and the sizzle of the coal-fired centre as the liquid is disturbed and hits a fresh hot spot. The very best bit is watching that guy who does not play well with others trying to keep a mad eye on all the bits that HE put in the steamboat and hovering over the broth to ensure no one else snaffles them. You can tell a lot about people by the way they eat and nothing breaks the ice like a crazy symphony of chopsticks, arms everywhere, and seeing that guy give up coveting and instead begin fishing vegies out for others and topping up their plates. I love it.

1 Soak the kombu in 1 litre of water for 30 minutes.

2 Arrange the carrot, cabbage, tofu, bok choy, spring onion and mushrooms on a platter or two. Cover with plastic film and refrigerate until required.

3 For the dipping sauce, use a mortar and pestle or food processor to grind the sesame seeds to a juicy paste. (This may take a while but it is worth the effort to achieve the pure flavour profile.) Transfer to a bowl and stir in the mirin, sugar, rice vinegar, soy sauce and garlic. Add the shiitake stock, stirring well. Divide the sauce among small bowls.

4 Fill the chimney of the steamboat cooker with small pieces of charcoal and light it. Add the kombu with its soaking water and the shiitake stock. Heat, removing the kombu just before the water comes to a boil. If you don't have a steamboat, simply use a cast iron pot and a table burner.

5 Place the cooker (or pot and burner) on the table along with the steamed rice, vegetables, tofu and bowls of dipping sauce. Swish the veg and tofu around in the stock until lightly cooked, then dip into the sauce. When all the vegetables have been eaten, drink up the delicious stock. ◖

Tomato, spinach AND haloumi risotto

1 × 400 g tin crushed tomatoes, juice strained and reserved

⅓ cup (80 ml) olive oil

4 golden shallots, diced

3 cloves garlic, crushed

6 sprigs marjoram or oregano, leaves picked

1 cup (200 g) arborio rice

⅓ cup (80 ml) dry white wine

salt flakes and cracked black pepper

150 g haloumi, cut into 5 mm thick slices

½ bunch English spinach, leaves chopped

60 g unsalted butter, chopped

grated zest and juice of 1 lemon

2 handfuls of flat-leaf parsley leaves

There's nothing wrong with getting your tomatoes out of a tin once summer is over (or, better, a jar if you have planned ahead). If you do grow your own, however, this dish is a great way to use up those tomatoes that stubbornly refused to ripen. Simply hang them upside-down in the shed and – voila – your last few stragglers will come good.

This risotto is light on butter because with the haloumi it can just become too much. I always try to put each part of a dish in context with the other components when I'm cooking, balancing the fat and salt contents while considering what else is going in later, so be prepared to be a little underwhelmed with the risotto until it all comes together at the end.

Although carnaroli is considered the king of risotto rice due to its creaminess, I use arborio here. This is for the same reason stated above: the haloumi already brings a degree of creaminess to the dish and I don't feel the expense is justified – but, if you have money to burn, by all means buy the fancy stuff.

1 Place the juice from the tinned tomatoes in a saucepan with 800 ml of water. Bring to a simmer over low heat and cover with a lid to keep warm.

2 Preheat a saucepan or saute pan over medium heat. Add 2 tablespoons of olive oil and saute the shallot for a minute or two, then add the garlic and marjoram or oregano and fry until softened. Add the rice and stir to coat with the oil; if it seems dry, add a little more oil. Toast the rice for a couple of minutes, then turn the heat up to high. Wait a few seconds, then deglaze with the wine and add a teaspoon or so of salt. When the wine has evaporated, add ½ cup (125 ml) of the hot tomato water and reduce the heat to medium–low. Stir, and when the liquid has been absorbed, add another ½ cup (125 ml) of hot tomato water. Continue in this way for about 15 minutes or until the rice is al dente and all the liquid has been absorbed.

3 Heat a chargrill pan over medium–high heat. Brush the haloumi with the remaining olive oil and grill for 2–3 minutes each side or until golden. When cool, tear up into bite-sized chunks.

4 Add the spinach, butter, lemon zest and juice to the rice and stir through until the spinach has wilted.

5 Serve the risotto topped with haloumi and parsley leaves. ◗

Mustard leaf saag <u>WITH</u> yoghurt-baked haloumi

350 g haloumi

100 g natural yoghurt

60 g ghee

2 onions, diced

4 cloves garlic, crushed

1 teaspoon freshly grated turmeric

2 teaspoons cumin seeds

1 tablespoon ground coriander

1 teaspoon fenugreek seeds

1 tablespoon poppy seeds

1 big bunch mustard leaf, roughly chopped

½ bunch English spinach, leaves roughly chopped

salt flakes

100 g butter, diced

½ large green chilli, sliced

pappadams and steamed basmati rice, to serve

Zingy and peppery, mustard leaf is the easiest vegie in the world to grow and it just keeps on giving. It is also readily available from Asian grocers. The liberal addition of butter to the puree takes the edge off the heat that would otherwise take over here. You could of course use paneer in this Indian dish, but I suggest you seek out a cow's milk haloumi and try it. We have some wonderful local cheesemakers and I can highly recommend Victoria McClurg's Barossa Valley Cheese Company's haloumi for this recipe.

1 Preheat the oven to 200°C fan-forced (220°C conventional) and lightly grease a baking tray. Break up the haloumi into chunks and smear with the yoghurt. Place on the baking tray and bake for 5–7 minutes until the yoghurt is dark brown with a few crispy bits.

2 Heat the ghee in a large heavy-based saucepan with a lid. Saute the onion and garlic over medium heat for 3–4 minutes or until softened. Increase the heat to medium–high, add the turmeric, cumin, coriander, fenugreek and poppy seeds and fry for 30 seconds or so until aromatic. (Be careful not to burn the fenugreek or it will become bitter – if the pan gets too hot, add a tablespoon of water to cool it down.)

3 Add the mustard leaf, spinach and ½ cup (125 ml) of water to the pan and toss to coat in the spices. Cover with the lid and cook for 3 minutes or until the greens have wilted. Check the seasoning, adding salt to taste, then puree with a stick blender, adding the butter while the mixture is hot.

4 Toss the haloumi on top of the saag. Garnish with green chilli and serve with pappadams and basmati rice. ◖

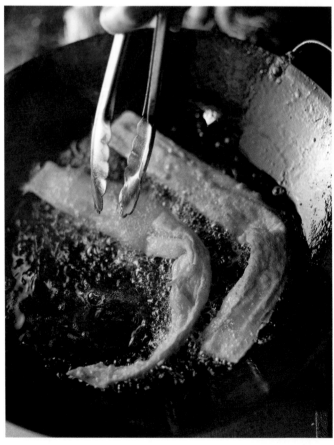

Char kway teo
WITH rice noodles

80 g beancurd sticks
(see Ingredients), soaked
in cold water for 1 hour

vegetable oil, for frying

4 free-range eggs

1 tablespoon sambal oelek

1 large onion, sliced

4 cloves garlic, crushed

½ teaspoon white sugar

1 bunch Chinese broccoli,
stems cut into 3 cm lengths
and leaves sliced in half

300 g firm tofu, ripped into
bite-sized pieces

⅓ cup (80 ml) light soy sauce

2 tablespoons dark soy sauce

¼ cup (60 ml) kecap manis

1 bunch garlic chives, cut into
3 cm lengths

½ bunch spring onions, green parts
cut into 3 cm batons

¼ teaspoon cracked white pepper

2 cups (160 g) bean sprouts

Rice noodles

vegetable oil, for greasing

1 cup (200 g) rice flour

½ cup (65 g) tapioca flour

This is a Chinese workers' dish, and the recipe traditionally starts with a slab of pork fat rendering in the wok. I've skipped that bit here and substituted over-fried beancurd sticks in place of the crispy pork (see below opposite). They have a crackling-like texture that is sensational and definitely worth the faff around.

The rice noodles are so simple to make (see opposite). The rice flour gives you the bite to the noodle and the tapioca the slippery silk, so you can muck around with ratios until you have your own signature style. The technique of adding only a third of the water to the batter and mixing it vigorously before adding the rest is simple food science. The starch in the flours need to be exploited or the noodles will break up later in the wok. The way to activate the starch is through motion and heat. If you have a dense batter when you start whisking, you can achieve this. If all the water goes in the batter at the outset, it's like trying to whisk water! Nothing happens: no friction, no heat and the starch just swirls and bobs around like a single paper boat in miles and miles of lonely ocean.

The absolute non-negotiable for this dish is to slightly char the rice noodles at the end. It's an easy technique to master as the starch really wants to catch and blister in the screaming hot wok; the addition of a little sugar helps this along.

1 For the rice noodles, set a steamer on top of a saucepan of water over medium heat. Grease a shallow cake tin (between 20 cm and 30 cm diameter is good; just make sure it fits in the steamer) with a little oil. Grease a large plate and set it aside. Combine the rice flour and tapioca flour in a bowl. Add ½ cup (125 ml) of water and vigorously work into a thick batter, about a minute or so. Slowly stream in another 1 cup (250 ml) of water, while whisking to combine.

2 Place the cake tin in the steamer for a minute to preheat. Re-whisk the noodle batter and pour it into the tin until about 2 mm thick. Swirl the tin using tongs to distribute the batter evenly. Pop the lid on the steamer and steam for about 2 minutes until the batter turns from cloudy to shiny and opaque. Remove from the heat and leave the batter to set for a minute, then gently peel it away from the tin and lay it on the greased plate. Repeat, whisking the batter well in between batches (as the flour will sink to the bottom) and ensuring the cake tin is kept warm and well-greased. Lay the noodle sheets on top of each other, lightly brushing with oil between layers. When cool, cut the sheets into 2 cm wide noodles and pile up on a tray.

Char kway teo WITH rice noodles *(cont.)*

3 Hold the soaked beancurd sticks upright and shake out any excess water, then pat them dry. Preheat 2–3 cups (500–750 ml) of vegetable oil in a large wok until just shimmering. Carefully pop in one or two sticks at a time, standing back as they fizz and splutter. Fry for about 1–2 minutes until crispy and golden brown, then remove and drain on paper towel. Repeat with the remaining beancurd sticks. When cool, break the fried sticks into 3–4 cm lengths. Discard the oil.

4 Return the wok to high heat and add 150 ml of vegetable oil. Crack two of the eggs into the oil, then pop the yolks and leave until almost set. Add half the sambal oelek and onion, and stir-fry for a few seconds, then add half the garlic. Once the onion is soft and the garlic is nutty, add half the rice noodles and sugar and stir a few times. Try and leave the noodles to char and blister – resist the urge to stir too much! Add half the broccoli stems, tofu, fried beancurd pieces, soy sauces and kecap manis and continue stir-frying for a minute or so, then fold in half of the broccoli leaves, chives, spring onion, pepper and bean sprouts. Remove from the wok. Repeat with the remaining ingredients.

5 Serve immediately. ◑

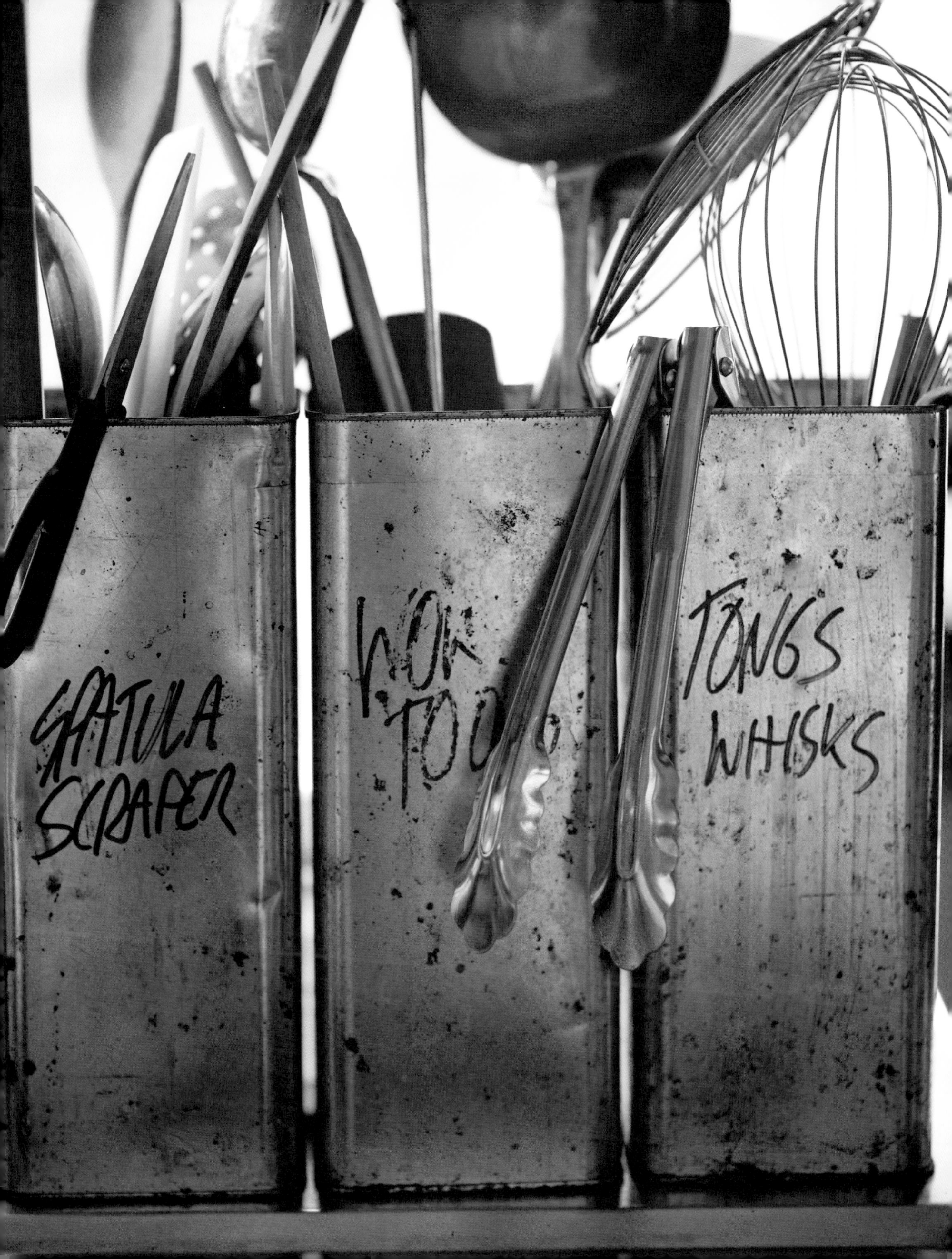
SPATULA
SCRAPER
WOK
TONGS
WHISKS

Smoky kale carbonara

50 g butter

4 golden shallots, thinly sliced

2 cloves garlic, crushed

1 cup (250 ml) white wine

300 ml pouring cream

4 free-range egg yolks, lightly beaten

100 g parmesan, grated

salt flakes and cracked black pepper

500 g bucatini or other thick spaghetti

Smoky kale chips

1 bunch kale, ribs and stems removed

1 tablespoon olive oil

1 teaspoon smoked paprika

¼ teaspoon salt flakes

Kale: I like it, but I absolutely love it like no other vegie when it's baked, crunchy and a little smoky. By wetting the kale before oiling and baking it, you will get super-crispy leaves but you need to be prepared to cook beyond where you want to stop! Be guided by crispness not colour.

And yup, I'll probably upset a million purists by referring to a dish without bacon as a 'carbonara' but there are so many stories about the origin of that one, I'll let the food geeks fight it out. Besides, it's not that I don't respect tradition – believe me I do. It's just that if something tastes good I don't mind what it's called, and I couldn't think of a better name for a dish containing parmesan, bucatini, eggs and black pepper, together a perfect blend of smokiness and creaminess.

1 For the smoky kale chips, preheat the oven to 180°C fan-forced (200°C conventional) and line two baking trays with baking paper. Pop the kale leaves in some water, then remove and shake them dry a little. Place the damp kale, olive oil, smoked paprika and salt in a large bowl and toss until well combined. Spread the kale over the prepared trays and bake for 12–15 minutes or until browned around the edges and crisp. Break the kale chips up a little and set them aside.

2 Melt the butter in a large saute pan or saucepan over medium heat. Add the shallot and saute for 5 minutes or until golden, then add the garlic and fry for a further 2 minutes. Deglaze with the wine and cook for a minute or so until reduced by half. Add the cream and cook for a further 2–3 minutes to reduce and thicken. Remove from the heat and allow the sauce to cool for a minute or two, then whisk in the egg yolks and parmesan. Season with salt and pepper.

3 Meanwhile, cook the spaghetti in a large saucepan of salted boiling water until al dente. Drain, then coat with the sauce.

4 To serve, divide the spaghetti among plates or bowls and top with the smoky kale chips.

Cocoa, lentil AND spelt brownies

30 g brown lentils (see Ingredients)

150 g unsalted butter, melted

1 cup (100 g) unsweetened cocoa powder (natural or Dutch-process)

1¼ cups (275 g) dark brown sugar

½ teaspoon salt flakes

3 large free-range eggs

½ teaspoon vanilla extract

1 cup (150 g) spelt flour

1 teaspoon baking powder

¼ cup (25 g) cocoa nibs, ground in a spice grinder

1 cup (110 g) walnut pieces

These brownies sound absolutely frightening, I know, but they are awesome. If you don't tell anyone there are lentils hiding inside, they will never know and just fall in love with them. A note about chocolate, cocoa nibs and cocoa powder. In the chocolate-making process, the cocoa butter and cocoa mass are split and extra cocoa butter is added back into the cocoa mass. This gives chocolate its creamy mouthfeel (along with vanilla, sugar and, if it's not good chocolate, milk powder, vegetable oil and lecithin). Cocoa nibs, however, have a naturally occurring ratio of cocoa butter to cocoa mass. Cocoa powder meanwhile has no or very little cocoa butter. Cocoa nibs are easy to find pre-ground or whole (which you can simply grind up in a spice grinder). You may want to try a health-food store or wholefood shop that makes a point of supplying foods as nature intended – exactly what the nibs are.

1 Place the lentils and 140 ml of water in a small saucepan and bring to a gentle simmer. Cover with a lid and simmer for 35 minutes. Leave to cool slightly, then place the lentils and their cooking liquid in a food processor and pulse until smooth, adding a tablespoon or so of extra water if necessary. You should end up with about ½ cup of lentil puree.

2 Preheat the oven to 175°C fan-forced (195°C conventional) and grease a slice tin (about 30 cm × 22 cm is good).

3 Place the lentil puree in a bowl with the melted butter, cocoa powder, sugar and salt and stir to combine well. Add the eggs one at a time, beating well after each addition. Stir in the vanilla, flour, baking powder, cocoa nibs and walnuts.

4 Spoon the batter into the prepared tin and smooth the surface. Bake for about 20 minutes or until a skewer inserted into the centre comes out clean. Cut into slices about 7 cm × 5 cm. The brownies will keep for a week in a sealed container in the fridge. ◖

Banana pops
WITH bee pollen

4 medium–large eco bananas

200 g couverture dark chocolate
(70 per cent cocoa), grated

2 tablespoons bee pollen

Freezing banana is a cheat's way of achieving a sorbet-like texture without mucking around with blitzing fruit, ice-cream churns and tons of sugar. (It's also not a bad way to deal with sweet persimmons if you have ever wondered what to do with an autumn glut of these wonderful fruits.) Speaking of unnecessary processes, many sweet snacks contain soy lecithin, which, as well as being an emulsifying agent, adds an unbelievable 'hyper' lubrication and lush palate. Whether that is good or bad, I'll leave up to you to decide, but you should know that bee pollen does a similar thing in fattening out flavour, plus it is high in protein, has a wonderful floral aroma (surprise, surprise) and tastes like a mouthful of slightly acidic lollies!

I am truly blessed to have 10 000 amazing girls sharing my backyard (get your mind out of the gutter – it's a beehive). I've popped a little brush on their hive entrance, which knocks a little pollen off their little legs each time they enter and when they're pulling truckloads home in spring, I gather it for a few days. I'm sure the bees hate me like the taxman I am for doing it, but I fill a little jar and store it in the fridge for special and whimsical dishes like this one. Bee pollen is also readily available from health food shops.

You don't have to temper the chocolate. Just melt it if you can't be bothered, but you will miss out on the glossy sheen and snap in your mouth if you don't.

1 Line a baking tray with baking paper. Either peel the bananas completely and insert a wooden pop stick into each one, or partially peel them, keeping the last few centimetres of skin attached (whatever – as long as you can hold the banana without getting chocolatey fingers). Arrange on the tray, cover with plastic film and place in the freezer for 3 hours or until frozen.

2 Once the bananas are frozen, place two-thirds of the chocolate in a heatproof bowl set over a saucepan of gently simmering water. Make sure no liquid touches the chocolate, as this will cause it to clump. Melt gently until the chocolate reaches 45°C – it's really important not to exceed this temperature, so a good thermometer is essential here. Remove from the heat and allow the chocolate to cool to 27°C, then add the remaining chocolate and stir through. Return it briefly to the heat until the chocolate reaches 32°C. Once all the chocolate has melted, it's ready to use.

3 Dip the bananas into the chocolate and hold upside down to allow the excess to drip off. Just as the chocolate is starting to set, sprinkle it with bee pollen. When the chocolate is set, it will have that telltale gloss and 'snap' in the mouth, so eat up! ◖

Salt-baked celeriac
<u>with</u> apple remoulade

²/₃ cup (100 g) plain flour

170 g cooking salt

2 tablespoons extra virgin olive oil

6 preserved vine leaves

1 large celeriac, peeled, leaves nipped off 2.5 cm from the top, bottom quarter sliced off and cut into fine matchsticks

1 red apple, cut into fine matchsticks

juice of 1 lemon

salt flakes

1 celery stick, cut into fine matchsticks

¼ cup (75 g) Egg-yolk mayonnaise (see Basics) or good-quality bought mayo

handful of flat-leaf parsley leaves, roughly chopped

½ cup (50 g) walnuts, toasted and lightly crushed

melba toasts, to serve (optional)

Without a doubt, this is the ultimate way to eat a celeriac. The easy-to-prepare salt dough imparts seasoning (the celeriac is protected from over-salting by a wrapping of vine leaves), holds the moisture during baking and looks brilliant – a great visual statement on the table. When you crack open the dough at the end, it reveals wisps of steam and super-creamy celeriac flesh with an intense flavour. Add a classic side of remoulade made with the celeriac trimmings and apple and the whole dish is a celebration of pure, simple flavours.

Photographer Alan Benson, who took the snaps for this book, is an all-round nice guy and a legend with the camera, but pretty hard to impress. After all, he has collaborated with many of Australia's great chefs. But after tasting this even Alan let out a little nod, maybe a quiet squeal (I made that bit up), and asked for the recipe. I'll take that as the ultimate compliment.

1 Preheat the oven to 210°C fan-forced (230°C conventional).

2 Place the flour and salt in a large bowl and mix until well combined. Add 90 ml of water and combine to form a stiff dough. On a lightly floured surface, roll the dough into a 20 cm round. Brush the dough with the oil, leaving 2.5 cm at the edges; this will prevent the vine leaves from sticking and allow the baked dough to be removed easily. Place the vine leaves over the dough, overlapping them to cover completely. Place the celeriac upright onto the vine leaves, then wrap it up in the dough, sealing at the top where the dough is unoiled and crimping around the tufts of stem.

3 Bake for 10 minutes, then reduce the temperature to 180°C fan-forced (200°C conventional) and bake for a further 2 hours or until you can easily pierce the celeriac with a skewer and it is soft and mushy in the centre.

4 While the celeriac is baking, make the remoulade. Sprinkle the celeriac and apple matchsticks with half the lemon juice and season with salt. Add the celery and mayonnaise and combine well, then sprinkle with the parsley and walnuts.

5 Crack open the salt-baked celeriac at the table – the salt dough should come away clean and can be discarded. Squeeze the remaining lemon juice over the top. Serve with the remoulade and, if you like, melba toasts as the baked celeriac flesh will be lovely and spreadable. ●

Cheddar AND mushroom fondue

2 cups (240 g) coarsely grated cheddar

1 heaped tablespoon cornflour

30 g butter

125 g pine or field mushrooms, chopped

1½ cups (375 ml) dry sparkling wine, plus a splash for deglazing

1 clove garlic, peeled

1 golden shallot, finely diced

salt flakes and cracked black pepper

1 tablespoon dijon mustard

1 tablespoon chopped chives

good sourdough bread, cut into bite-sized pieces, to serve

pickles, to serve

baby veg, to serve

Fondue is my number-one food memory. As far as I can recall, at some point in the 1970s we had one of those dinner-menu rosters stuck to the fridge. We also had a fondue set, which I thought was the most exotic thing in the known universe. (I had heard it was a Swedish thing. If you were ten in 1975, you probably would've thought Abba and therefore obviously anything Swedish was pretty exciting too.) We each had an allocated fondue fork with a different coloured tip and every week the argument would begin afresh about who owned which fork (five brothers will do that). The free-for-all over a piece of bread that fell off someone's fork into the fondue pot was terrifying because it was instantly classified finder's keepers.

I fondly remember everything about those meals – the smells, the conversations, the visitors, the usual sibling rivalry. I put this down to the magic that is a completely dysfunctional family sharing a meal. There were never TV dinners in our house: we always ate at the table and the food was always cooked, always served family-style. For this I am truly grateful to my parents, who were often tired from work and yet still maintained what was a disappearing tradition. When convenience meals started appearing with their lonely little portion-controlled meanness, I believe we lost so much more than health and nutrition: we lost ownership and pride in our food preparation and we lost the table. I wouldn't trade my childhood memories of those times around the table for the world and I really wish I still had my red fondue fork.

Oh, and the secret to a good fondue? Well, we are producing some stunning sparkling white wines in Australia and the recipe only requires half a bottle, so buy the best dry bubbles you can afford and drink the rest while you are cooking.

1 Place the cheddar and cornflour in a clean plastic bag and shake to combine.

2 Heat the butter in a small frying pan over medium heat. Add the mushrooms and fry for 8–10 minutes until a little dark and crispy. Deglaze with a splash of sparkling wine.

3 Rub the base and sides of a heavy-based saucepan with the garlic clove, then discard the garlic. Add the sparkling wine and half of the shallot and place the pan over medium heat for 2 minutes or until the wine boils.

4 Remove the pan from the heat and rain in the cheddar and cornflour mixture, distributing it evenly across the surface and whisking it in as it melts and thickens. Return the fondue to low heat and season with salt and pepper. Make sure the mixture does not boil. Add the fried mushrooms and the mustard, stirring until well combined.

5 Sprinkle over the chives and serve with bread, pickles and baby veg. ◑

Beets, green lentils AND crispy skin garlic

1 bunch red baby beets, trimmed

1 bunch target baby beets, trimmed

1 bunch orange baby beets, trimmed

2 tablespoons extra virgin olive oil

100 g pitted kalamata olives

1 head garlic, cloves separated

salt flakes and cracked black pepper

grated zest of 1 lemon

Green lentils

300 g French-style green lentils (see Ingredients)

1 bay leaf

3 sprigs thyme

150 g butter

½ celeriac, diced

½ leek, white part only, diced

½ celery stick, diced

100 ml verjuice or white wine

salt flakes

In the cooler months a crazy array of beets hits the markets. I like 'em all: the peppery orange guys, the sweet red babies, the targets with their little bull's eyes. In this dish, the beets are simmered and then sauteed to really bring out their sweetness. (For this reason I'd avoid using the light-red candy beets here as they can get a little too sweet.) The beets provide a nice contrast to the subtle straw flavour of the French-style green lentils, which we happen to grow very well in Australia these days.

1 Brush or gently scrape the tops of the beets clean, then place them in a large saucepan of salted cold water and bring to a simmer over medium heat. Cook for 20 minutes or until tender, then drain and cut into bite-sized pieces.

2 For the lentils, place them in a saucepan with 1.2 litres of cold water and the bay leaf and thyme. Bring to a gentle simmer over medium heat and cook for 30 minutes or until the lentils are tender and nestled in a scant amount of liquid. Set aside and keep warm.

3 Preheat the oven to 180°C fan-forced (200°C conventional). Place the olive oil, olives and garlic on a baking tray and season with salt and pepper. Roast for 15 minutes, then add the beets and stir to coat in the oil. Cook for a further 15 minutes or until the garlic has crispy skin and is mushy on the inside and the olives begin to shrivel slightly.

4 Meanwhile, heat a heavy-based frying pan over medium heat and add the butter. When it starts to sizzle, add the celeriac and leek and fry for a few minutes, then fold in the celery and cook for a further 3 minutes until soft. Add the verjuice or wine and season with salt, then turn up the heat to reduce the liquid for a minute or so. Pour the lot onto the cooked lentils and stir through.

5 To serve, place the lentils in a bowl with their liquid and scatter with the olives, garlic and beets. Garnish with lemon zest. ◑

Kimchi, spring onion AND hot pepper soup

4 spring onions, white and green parts separated

1 teaspoon sesame oil

¼ cup (60 ml) flavour-neutral oil (see page 33)

3 cm ginger, peeled and cut into matchsticks

2 cloves garlic, crushed

1 small onion, sliced

1 tablespoon white sugar

2 tablespoons Korean hot pepper paste

⅓ cup (80 ml) light soy sauce

300 g fresh udon noodles

300 g silken tofu, in 3 cm cubes

Kimchi

1 Chinese cabbage, cut into 2 cm cubes

1 tablespoon salt flakes

1 teaspoon chilli flakes

1 teaspoon rice vinegar

4 spring onions, green parts cut into 4 cm batons

1 cup (80 g) bean sprouts

2 cloves garlic, crushed

1 teaspoon soy sauce

1 tablespoon white sugar

Kimchi is something you should have a pop at, at least once. (In fact, you may well have to do it yourself if you are vego or vegan as most commercially produced jars contain fish.) Full-blown lactic fermentation can take 3 weeks at normal room temperature. However, I am often far too impatient to wait that long, so this recipe uses a wing-it version that takes just days. It still has some probiotic benefits, as well as plenty of flavour. I usually leave the kimchi out at room temp for 4 days (but try 2 weeks if your house is a winter tomb) to achieve enough funkiness, then I pop it in the fridge to stop any further fermentation. The correct way to start kimchi is to press the excess moisture out of the cabbage, but instead I salt a little heavier than other recipes, another shortcut that produces a decent result. A cautionary note: there is a big difference between encouraging fermentation and adding bugs by way of cross-contamination, so clean hands and sterilised jars are still important.

The soup itself has a subtle smoky flavour (achieved by almost obliterating the spring onions on a chargrill plate), which plays nicely with the accompanying chilli, vinegar and sugar. The tofu and noodles then bolster the broth into a filling meal.

1 For the kimchi, place the cabbage in a large bowl or spread it out over a tray. Sprinkle with salt and rub it in gently without damaging the leaves. Leave for 30 minutes or so; water should start to gather in the bowl or tray. Redistribute the salt and cabbage and leave for a further hour.

2 Meanwhile, soak the chilli flakes in the rice vinegar.

3 Remove the cabbage and discard the water. Rinse the cabbage really well, then drain and gently shake off excess water while squeezing. Try not to destroy the cabbage with too much pressure – a 'firm handshake' with your cabbage will do it.

4 Place the drained cabbage, spring onion and bean sprouts in a bowl and add the garlic, soy, sugar and chilli and vinegar. Stir until well combined.

5 Transfer the kimchi to a 1–1.5 litre sterilised jar and leave on your benchtop: after 4 days, have a taste and decide whether it is 'funky' enough for you. Once the kimchi has achieved your desired level of fermentation, pop it in the fridge. It will keep for months – just keep an eye out for mould; if it appears, you'll need to ditch the batch.

Kimchi, spring onion AND
hot pepper soup (cont.)

6 Place a chargrill pan over medium–high heat. Add the spring onion whites and sesame oil and chargrill until smoky, blistered and tender. Remove from the heat and leave to cool, then slice the spring onion into thirds and set aside.

7 Heat the oil in a large saucepan over medium heat and add the ginger, garlic and onion. Saute for 3–4 minutes, then add the sugar. Add the pepper paste, soy sauce and 3 cups (750 ml) of water and bring to a simmer, then add the noodles and leave them to warm through. Remove from the heat and add ⅔ cup (180 g) of kimchi, the white and green spring onion and the tofu.

8 Divide the soup among bowls and serve.

Brown rice AND walnut dolmades

1 cup (250 ml) extra virgin olive oil

2 large onions, finely diced

6 spring onions, white parts finely sliced

2 cloves garlic, finely chopped

1 cup (200 g) medium-grain brown rice

⅓ cup (55 g) currants

⅓ cup (35 g) walnuts, chopped

handful of finely chopped mint

handful of finely chopped flat-leaf parsley

small handful of finely chopped dill

½ teaspoon finely grated lemon zest

juice of 2 lemons

300 g preserved vine leaves, rinsed

Some dolmades taste like tin – probably because they came out of one – but these are fantastic little bundles of flavour. I love chewing through a vine leaf or two on my way to the rice inside. Everything about brown rice is okay by me. I like the sudden change of aroma in the kitchen when it is just a few minutes away from being ready. I like eating it, and I like the sustained energy I get afterwards. It's a sort of clean feeling whereby you know your body is approving of the fuel you just popped in the tank.

I also like mindless repetition. In my opinion, it's totally underrated – jeez, who wants to think all the time? – and jobs like this allow you to just get busy and get on with it. I like to make each one better and faster, and I feel a little sad yet satisfied when the task is done. You probably think I am insane but the greater part of a chef's day is *mise en place* (setting up the ingredients) and when you are prepping for hundreds or even thousands of meals, making 50 dolmades is a walk in the park! Don't be fooled by all the images of chefs tossing pans around and screaming at each other: that's just showtime. A lot of chopping and folding and peeling occurred ten hours before you came for dinner. That's when the real work was done and you quickly learn to enjoy it if you make a career of cooking.

1 Heat half the olive oil in a large saute or frying pan over low heat. Add the onion, spring onion and garlic and stir well, then cover and cook for 5 minutes until the onion is translucent. Add the rice, currants, walnuts and 1 cup (250 ml) of water, stirring until well combined. Increase the heat and bring to the boil, then reduce the heat, cover and simmer for 10 minutes or until the water has been absorbed. Remove from the heat and leave the rice to cool for 10 minutes before adding the herbs and lemon zest and juice of 1 lemon. Stir until well combined.

2 Place a few vine leaves on a tea towel, flat-side down so the veins are facing upwards. Spoon 1–2 teaspoons of rice mixture into the centre of each leaf and roll up tightly from the stem end, bringing up the sides to enclose the filling. Repeat with the remaining filling and leaves, reserving a few leaves to line the base of the saucepan during cooking.

3 Place the reserved vine leaves in a large heavy-based saucepan. Tightly pack the dolmades, seam-side down, in a layer. Sprinkle with a couple of tablespoons of olive oil and lemon juice, then repeat the process to make several layers of dolmades. Place an inverted heatproof plate on top to keep them in place. Pour over 1–2 cups (250–500 ml) of water, then cover with a lid and bring to the boil. Reduce the heat to low and simmer for 30 minutes. Remove from the heat and leave the dolmades to cool to room temperature in their cooking liquid before serving. ◗

Blood orange AND fennel salad WITH harissa

1 fennel bulb, quartered and very finely sliced using a mandolin, fronds reserved for garnish

4 blood oranges (or navel oranges), peel left on, sliced horizontally into rounds, then quartered

2 carrots, cut into matchsticks

handful of dates, pitted and quartered

2 tablespoons ras el hanout

½ teaspoon icing sugar

70 ml extra virgin olive oil

grated zest and juice of 1 lemon

cracked black pepper

¼ cup (40 g) roasted almonds, roughly chopped

½ bunch coriander, leaves picked

mint sprigs, to garnish

couscous or flatbread, to serve (optional)

Harissa

4–6 small red chillies, seeds and all

2 chargrilled red capsicums (peppers) in oil

1 clove garlic, peeled

2 teaspoons coriander seeds, toasted

1 teaspoon cumin seeds

drizzle of olive oil

½ teaspoon salt flakes

I hadn't considered eating the white pithy part of the orange outside of a jar of marmalade, but this really – no, really – works in this dish. The oranges are sliced straight across, skin, pith, flesh, seeds and all. If you are using blood oranges, you get a free splash of colour and the fruit has a berry-ish sweetness. But a winter navel will also do as the blood orange season is short and the dish is definitely worth a try.

The dates counter the orange pith with their super sweetness. They were always a bit of an indulgence when I was growing up. My mum would come home with a big box of dates and it didn't take us long to work through their sticky, sweet, fibrous flesh. We do have some fresh dates being grown in Australia and they are a real surprise: they look like little shiny pale-yellow quail eggs and have a subtle creamy caramel flavour with a distinctly crunchy texture, unlike the jammy, chewy dried ones. The season draws to an end as autumn does, but the dates store well and you might just see some in early winter. I actually froze some a while back and they were perfect when thawed. Grab some and you will be rewarded.

1 To make the harissa, blend all the ingredients to a smooth paste in a food processor. Set aside.

2 Combine the fennel, orange, carrot and dates in a large bowl. Add the ras el hanout, icing sugar, olive oil, lemon zest and juice and mix to combine. Season with pepper.

3 Spoon the harissa over the top, then hit the salad with the almonds, fennel fronds, coriander and mint.

4 Serve with couscous or flatbread, if you like.

Jerusalem artichoke gnocchi <u>WITH</u> mushrooms <u>AND</u> cavolo nero

300 g pine or field mushrooms, cut into wedges

8 cloves garlic, skin on

140 ml verjuice

100 ml extra virgin olive oil

salt flakes and cracked black pepper

1 bunch cavolo nero, leaves roughly chopped

Jerusalem artichoke gnocchi

1 kg jerusalem artichokes, peeled

¼ cup (60 ml) olive oil

⅓ cup (25 g) finely grated parmesan

1 teaspoon salt flakes

1 free-range egg yolk

150 g wholemeal flour

2 tablespoons semolina flour

Otherwise known as 'Three of my favourite things'. Chefs tend to covet information about their best patches for collecting mushrooms. The conversation can become a little uneasy as two of them dance around each other trying to glean (and protect) secrets. The vibrant orange caps of pine mushrooms are fairly easy to spot, however. Go for a drive near a pine plantation and you'll often find an abundance of them along the roadside. Of course when it comes to collecting mushrooms, if you don't know what you're doing you need to skip the forest and visit a speciality grocer or mushroom providore instead. And if you can't get hold of pine mushrooms, you can always substitute field mushrooms.

Cavolo nero may translate to 'black cabbage' but, strictly speaking, it is a member of the kale family, which is headless and thus more closely related to wild cabbage than our modern, compact-headed soccer balls. I love it for its other-worldly appearance and how it blisters when exposed to high heat, but curly kale is fine as a substitute.

1 Preheat the oven to 200°C fan-forced (220°C conventional). For the gnocchi, place the artichokes in a baking dish with the olive oil and toss until well coated. Roast for 40 minutes or until golden. Transfer to a food processor and pulse to a smooth puree. Place in a large bowl with the parmesan, salt, egg yolk and enough wholemeal flour to bind (you may not need it all). Knead until you have a dry, doughy consistency; add a little water if it's too dry, or flour if it's too wet. Divide the dough into three. On a floured surface, roll the dough into long sausages, then cut into 2.5 cm pieces. Spread the semolina flour over a tray, add the gnocchi and leave in the fridge for 20 minutes.

2 Meanwhile, place the mushrooms and garlic on a baking tray and pour over ⅓ cup (80 ml) of verjuice and 2 tablespoons of olive oil. Season with salt and pepper and mix well. Roast for about 20 minutes until well coloured.

3 Turn off the oven and oil a baking tray. Place a large saucepan of salted water over low heat and maintain a gentle simmer. Working in batches, cook the gnocchi until they float, then remove with a slotted spoon and place on the oiled tray. Be careful that the water neither boils rapidly (as the gnocchi will break up), nor gets too cool (as they will swell too much). Pop the gnocchi in the oven with the door ajar; the residual heat will keep them warm.

4 Heat the remaining olive oil in a frying pan over medium–low heat. Add the cavolo nero, season with salt and pepper and saute for 5 minutes until tender. Deglaze the pan with the remaining verjuice and cook for a further minute or so until reduced by half. Add the roasted mushrooms and garlic and warm through. Place the cavolo nero, mushrooms and garlic in a large bowl, add the gnocchi and gently combine. Serve immediately. ●

Broccoli AND gruyere fritters

2 heads broccoli, chopped into florets, stems roughly sliced

1 cup (150 g) plain flour

2 teaspoons cumin seeds

200 g gruyere, coarsely grated

large handful of flat-leaf parsley leaves, chopped

½ teaspoon salt flakes

3 free-range eggs, lightly beaten

1 cup (250 ml) extra virgin olive oil

1 lemon, halved

Finger food with substance, these very moreish fritters work particularly well as a part of a stand-up party spread. They are also perfect for kids who allege they don't like anything healthy, green or even remotely vegie-related. Even though the broccoli is on the crunchy side here, its presence is toned down by the gruyere, which gives a stretchy, gooey texture and a hint of nutty sweetness.

For those of you chasing a gluten-free version, I am pleased to report a batch I made using chickpea (besan) flour worked perfectly, with the only addition being a teaspoon of baking powder to relieve the flour of its characteristic density.

1 Place the broccoli florets and stems, flour, cumin seeds, gruyere, parsley, salt and eggs in a food processor. Pulse until well combined and starting to ball up.

2 With floured hands, form the broccoli and gruyere mixture into 6 cm × 2 cm patties, pressing together so the ingredients are well compacted. You should have enough to make about 16 patties.

3 Heat the olive oil in a large non-stick frying pan over medium heat until shimmering. Working in batches, fry the fritters for 3–4 minutes on each side or until golden brown.

4 Serve the fritters with a squeeze of lemon. ◑

Serves 4

Hot pot with the lot

¼ cup (about 10 g) dried shiitake mushrooms, soaked overnight in cold water

4 or 5 dried lotus root slices, soaked overnight in cold water

1 piece cloud ear fungus (see Ingredients), soaked overnight in cold water

1 piece wood fungus (see Ingredients), soaked overnight in cold water

¼ cup (about 30 g) dried jujube, soaked overnight in cold water

2 cups (500 ml) vegetable oil

5 g beancurd sticks (see Ingredients), broken into 5 cm lengths

4 cloves garlic, crushed

2 tablespoons (about 25 g) chopped brown beans

¼ cup (60 ml) shaohsing

10 g sweet beancurd sticks (see Ingredients)

2 tablespoons (about 15 g) dried lily flowers, knotted, soaked overnight in cold water

¼ cup (60 ml) dark soy sauce

10 g goji berries

2 tablespoons (about 40 g) rock candy

5 g black moss (bamboo fungus)

2 tablespoons (about 50 g) fermented white bean cheese

¼ cup (60 ml) hoisin sauce

2 tablespoons cornflour mixed with ⅓ cup (80 ml) water

steamed jasmine rice, to serve

This one is going out to all the people I see hovering nervously around the dried goods section at Asian grocers, looking like they want to have a play but don't quite know how to start. This section, usually found in a challenging corner of the store, contains a dazzling array of baffling dried delicacies and pungent aromas. Sure, this dish may be out of your comfort zone, but set a Saturday morning aside for the shop and the afternoon for a cook-up and you will have an adventure that is both rewarding and memorable. The dried ingredients really aren't that scary and provide a myriad of textures for the adventurous cook.

From the top . . . Cloud ear fungus is a thin, black mushroom with a frilly edge, and a fairly light texture. Wood fungus is heavier and thicker (about the thickness of dried tangerine peel) than cloud ear, with a white underside and a black top side. Dried lotus roots look like little white mag wheels: they have a spoke pattern from slicing across the grooves that run the length of the semi-hollow lotus root. Lily flowers don't look like flowers, but like pale-yellow little worms around 50 cm long. Jujube or Chinese red date vary in size from 5 to 50 cents, largely due to degree of drying. Rock candy, a sugar with bigger crystals, looks like large (5–20 mm) yellow rocks. Black moss is a lichen and looks like coarse black hair. Fermented white bean cheese comes in jars; it looks like little cubes of cheese and can only be described as pungent and complex.

1 Remove and discard the shiitake mushroom stems and cut the caps into wedges. Cut the lotus root into wedges. Slice the cloud ear and wood fungus. Pit and slice the jujube. Set them all aside.

2 Heat the oil in a wok over high heat. Add the broken beancurd sticks and fry for about 30 seconds to 1 minute until they blister up, then remove with a spider or slotted spoon. Discard all but 100 ml of the cooking oil. Chop the fried beancurd sticks into bite-sized pieces and then place them in 1 cup (250 ml) of water for about 30 minutes to soften.

3 Add the shiitake and lotus root to the wok and fry in the reserved oil over medium heat for 2–3 minutes until coloured. Add the cloud and wood fungus, garlic and brown beans. Fry for about 1 minute until aromatic, then deglaze with the shaohsing. Add 1.2 litres of water and the jujube, fried soaked beancurd sticks, sweet beancurd sticks, lily flowers and soy sauce and simmer for 1 hour.

4 Add the goji berries, rock candy, black moss, bean cheese and hoisin. Whisk in a stream of the cornflour mixture and simmer for another 10 minutes or so until thick, like pumpkin soup.

5 Serve with steamed jasmine rice. ●

Masoor dal and roti

Dal

1 cup (200 g) split and hulled red lentils (see Ingredients)

2 cloves garlic, skin on, lightly bashed, plus 2 cloves garlic, minced

2–3 cm ginger, sliced into chunks, plus 1 tablespoon minced ginger

⅓ cup (80 ml) melted ghee or flavour-neutral oil (see page 33)

1 tablespoon cumin seeds

½ teaspoon brown mustard seeds

1 onion, chopped

1½ teaspoons chilli powder

2½ teaspoons ground coriander

1 teaspoon ground turmeric

salt flakes

juice of 1 large lemon

coriander leaves, to garnish

1–2 tablespoons ghee (extra; optional)

Roti

3 cups (450 g) roti (atta) flour or plain flour

1 tablespoon salt

2 teaspoons white sugar

2 tablespoons melted ghee or flavour-neutral oil

1 free-range egg, lightly beaten

1 cup (250 ml) flavour-neutral oil, plus a little extra for frying

I never tire of eating dal. I always cook a big batch and then every day I throw something different in the pan (spinach, pumpkin, potato) to mix it up a little. Dal literally means split legumes, which can be lentils, peas or beans. More often than not, the legumes are also hulled (the outer skin is removed), which further accelerates the already quick cooking time. I am all for whole food and it's true you lose a few nutritional goodies from the splitting and hulling, but what you gain is speed – vroom, vroom. What's more, this dal uses red lentils, one of the speediest to cook: just 15 minutes from when they hit a simmer until they acquire the requisite mushy, creamy texture. I reckon that's a pretty good trade-off and makes this super healthy, super fast food.

I often eat this with rice but when I am feeling enthusiastic I make a big batch of roti and freeze them raw between sheets of plastic film, then pan-fry them straight from the freezer for meals such as the Calcutta roll on page 200. It's a little bit of an episode to make roti so if you are going to bother – and once you have mastered the technique – throw an extra measure in the recipe and start a little production line. The dough is easy, but the spreading and booking of the dough is a little tricky (albeit a lot of fun) and the griddling method requires practice. However, it brings great rewards. The best part is folding the breads and smacking them to fluff up the pastry, creating the roti's signature flakiness. If you ever get a chance to see a true roti master throwing the dough, you will be mesmerised and probably tempted to have a shot at home. The method involves a complex procedure of crossing your arms, peeling the dough off the benchtop, getting it airborne and flicking it to stretch it out. I try to give this technique a pop every time I make roti and inevitably end up with a crumpled mess on the floor, ceiling, my arms and generally everywhere except the benchtop, but I will never give up because my failure still makes me laugh. Don't be put off though: this is my trainer-wheel recipe and it calls for you to simply squish and flatten the dough out on the benchtop – no acrobatics involved.

1 For the roti, sift the flour and salt together, add the sugar then rub in the ghee or oil. Combine the egg with 1 cup (250 ml) of warm water and add to the flour. Knead the dough for about 10 minutes until soft, smooth and elastic (or you can use a mixer for about 7 minutes on medium speed). Divide the dough into 10 balls and place them in a container with 1 cup (250 ml) of oil or enough to cover. Leave to rest at room temperature for at least an hour.

2 Meanwhile, for the dal, place the lentils in a saucepan with 1 litre of cold water and the whole garlic cloves and ginger chunks. Cook for about 25 minutes until soft and mushy. Toss out the garlic and ginger and set the lentils aside.

Masoor dal AND roti (cont.)

3 Heat the ghee or oil in a saucepan over medium heat. Add the cumin and mustard seeds and gently heat for a few seconds, stirring, until you can smell the cumin. Fold in the onion and fry for about 5 minutes until soft and lightly browned, then add the minced garlic and ginger and stir for 30 seconds. Add the chilli powder, ground coriander, turmeric and salt and fry for about 5 minutes, then add the lentils to the pan (you can also add more liquid to achieve the consistency you like) and leave to simmer for 5–6 minutes. Turn off the heat, pop a lid on and set the dal aside while you finish the roti; you can gently reheat it later if necessary.

4 Gently lift the dough balls out of the oil. Take one ball and spread the dough out in all directions with your palm, then roll to form a rectangle of about 45 cm × 30 cm. The dough will be see-through thin and a few holes will appear, but don't worry! Fold over a third of the longer edge at one side, and then a third at the other, then fold the whole thing in half at the short edge. The dough will want to pull back a little when you do this – gently stretching as you fold will ensure your final bread is 15 cm odd square. You will now have six layers of dough, and the residual oil between them will ensure each layer will puff up, creating lovely, flaky bread. Don't be tempted to re-roll the dough as the pressure will glue the layers together and impede its flakiness. Repeat with all the balls.

5 Preheat a heavy-based frying pan over medium heat and add ¼ teaspoon of oil, spreading it well over the bottom of the pan. Pop in the roti one at a time and leave for 30 seconds to a minute, then gently flip it over. At this stage, the surface will start to set. Now grab a tea towel and bunch it up so it is fist-sized and – very carefully so as not to burn yourself – dab the roti at about 10-second intervals all over the surface; this will ensure all the layers cook through and it will also crisp up the bottom. The roti will start expanding and puffing around the edges where you press with the tea towel. This is a good sign that the layers are cooking correctly and steaming through on the inside. Flip the roti, add a smidge more oil and repeat until the bread is set with pale, light-brown and dark-brown patches. Be careful not to add too much oil; you want just enough so that the bread is neither toasting nor (worse) frying, but somewhere in between. Remove the roti from the pan and lay it on the benchtop. Fold each corner into the middle of the bread, then invert and clap between your hands using an inward and upward action. The layers will partially peel apart and this gives the roti its characteristic fluffy and slightly broken texture. You will be left with a little upright parcel and some flaky crumbs. Repeat with the remaining roti.

6 When you are ready to serve the dal, add lemon juice and salt and sprinkle with coriander. If you like, you can also stir in extra ghee to really enrich the dal and fatten the flavour. Serve with the roti alongside. ◗

Serves 6

Calcutta roll (roti WITH egg, chilli AND coriander)

6 roti (see page 196)

70 ml ghee or flavour-neutral oil (see page 33)

3 small onions, sliced

3–4 cloves garlic, crushed

1 large red chilli, finely chopped (seeds and all)

heaped ½ teaspoon chat masala

6 free-range eggs

2 big handfuls of coriander, chopped

This recipe came about as we tested batches of roti (with varying amounts of sugar, ghee, salt and egg) for the Masoor dal on the previous pages. Jodie, who was an apprentice when I was a junior sous chef 15 or 20 years ago, is responsible for it. An absolute whizz with all things pastry and baking, Jodie is also a bit well-travelled and back in the day when she walked (and cooked) the earth, she saw this simple hawker snack being made in India. During testing, she knocked it up out of the reject rotis and the cookbook crew inhaled them. The recipe was declared an absolute winner and a worthy addition to the book. It's since become a bit of a go-to quick supper for me.

The roti is cooked with egg, then packed full of aromatics and zing from coriander, chilli and chat masala, which has a pronounced tang from a heavy dose of dried mango. This would also be great in spring with the addition of shredded iceberg lettuce and diced cucumber.

1 Make the roti according to the method on page 196, but once cooked, remove them from the frying pan and just stack them up on a plate (rather than creating the upright parcel shape described on page 199). Cover the stacked roti with a tea towel.

2 Place the frying pan back over medium heat. Add 2 tablespoons of ghee or oil and when hot add the onion and saute for a few minutes until soft and translucent. Add the garlic and chilli and continue to fry for a minute or two, stirring, then add the chat masala and stir to combine. Tip the spice mixture into a bowl and cover so the ingredients retain a little heat.

3 Return the pan to medium heat, add ½ teaspoon of ghee or oil and swirl the pan. Crack an egg into the pan, pop the yolk with a spatula and immediately place a roti on top; the egg will stick to the bottom of the roti as it cooks. Cook for a minute or two until the egg is just set, then remove with a spatula and invert onto your benchtop, egg-side up. Place a sixth of the spice mixture and a sixth of the coriander towards the edge of the roti and roll it up like a wrap. Repeat with the remaining roti and filling. ◗

Fennel AND star anise broth WITH soba noodles

250 g soba noodles

¼ cup (60 ml) flavour-neutral oil (see page 33)

pinch of cracked white pepper

1 baby fennel, finely sliced, reserving a few fronds for garnish

200 g silken firm tofu, in large chunks

a few drops of sesame oil

Stock

2 onions, roughly chopped

2 spring onions, white parts tied in knots, green parts chopped

4 cm ginger, sliced and bruised

1 star anise

½ cup (15 g) dried shiitake mushrooms

⅓ cup (80 ml) light soy sauce

2 tablespoons mirin

salt flakes

Fennel and star anise mirror each other and partner up brilliantly, and this broth is a pure magic. I am pretty keen on dishes where the trimmings go back into the preparation – in this case the stock – because it just seems so sensible.

It's a small thing, but frying the shiitakes and adding white pepper after they are poached gives them a completely new dimension. I am a firm believer in the little details. That's why I like to see a chef who smells, listens and looks as he fiddles with the pans on the hob, noting every change in the ingredients and pushing for that little ounce of extra flavour.

1 For the stock, combine the onion, spring onion whites, ginger, star anise, shiitakes and 1.5 litres of water in a large saucepan over high heat. Bring to the boil, then reduce the heat and simmer for 1 hour. Strain the stock, discarding the onion, spring onion, ginger and star anise but reserving the shiitakes. Cut off and discard the shiitake stems, then slice the caps and set them aside. Return the strained stock to the saucepan and add the soy sauce and mirin and salt to taste.

2 Boil the soba noodles in plenty of water according to the packet instructions, until just cooked or slightly underdone. Drain, then run under warm water to remove the starch. Set aside.

3 Place a small frying pan over high heat and add the oil. Fry the shiitakes to knock some colour onto them, then season with pepper.

4 Add the fried shiitakes to the stock, then place the pan over medium heat and add the fennel. Simmer for about 5 minutes, but not so long as to make the fennel mushy; you want a little texture.

5 Divide the soba noodles and tofu among four bowls and pour over the shiitake and fennel stock. Serve sprinkled with green spring onion, fennel fronds and sesame oil. ●

Borlotti bean ball minestrone

2 tablespoons olive oil, plus extra for drizzling

1 onion, diced

2 cloves garlic, crushed

1 carrot, diced

1 celery stick, diced

1 × 400 g tin crushed tomatoes

2 waxy potatoes (such as kipflers or bintjes), cut into 1.5 cm dice

50 g spaghetti, broken into 4 cm lengths

salt flakes and cracked black pepper

small handful of chopped flat-leaf parsley

shaved parmesan, to garnish

Borlotti bean balls

¾ cup (150 g) borlotti beans, soaked overnight in cold water

3–4 strips (about ½ whole) roasted red capsicum (pepper), roughly chopped

¼ small onion, grated

2 cloves garlic, crushed

small handful of chopped flat-leaf parsley

1 teaspoon dried oregano

1 free-range egg, lightly beaten

¼ cup (25 g) dried breadcrumbs

salt flakes and cracked black pepper

With a slab of crusty bread on the side (and maybe a decent salad) this soup can be a meal; without, it's a great lunch, supper or entree. It's one of those soups with enough happening that you feel satisfied eating it as the main event. The balls may seem like a bit of a fluff around, but it's nice to have something a little extra going on apart from the broth, the slippery strands of pasta and the diced vegies. They are quite delicate, so if you are chasing a meatball-type texture I suggest you throw in a little cornflour, work the mix really hard and press the balls tightly, then shallow-fry them.

That recurring 'extra drizzle' of olive oil is not to be dismissed as chef frivolity. Many of the health benefits and subtle flavours and aromas in good olive oils are at least partially lost to heat during cooking. So this is the time to grab your most coveted, secret stash of first-press or early-harvest oil and really let the dish sing. It is always the little things that make or break a dish.

1 For the borlotti bean balls, drain and rinse the beans, then place them in a saucepan with 2 cups (500 ml) of water. Bring to a simmer and cook for 45 minutes or until tender. (Top up the water if required but use as little as possible – you want the mixture to bind later.) Drain the beans really well, then return them to the pan and pop the lid on to keep them warm.

2 Preheat the oven to 180°C fan-forced (200°C conventional) and line a baking tray with baking paper. Place the beans in a food processor with the capsicum and pulse until smooth. Transfer to a large bowl and add the onion, garlic, parsley, oregano, egg and breadcrumbs, then season with salt and pepper. Bind the ingredients together using your hands, then take a tablespoon of the mixture and roll it into a ball. Repeat with the remaining mixture, placing the balls on the prepared tray as you go; you should end up with about 20. Bake for 15–20 minutes until they are light golden brown and firm. Turn the oven off and leave the door ajar to keep them warm.

3 Meanwhile, heat the olive oil in a large heavy-based saucepan over low heat and add the onion, garlic, carrot and celery. Cover with a lid and cook for a few minutes, then add the tomato, potato and 800 ml of water. Turn up the heat and bring to a simmer. Cook for 20 minutes or until the vegetables are tender. Add the spaghetti and cook for 7 minutes or until al dente. Season with salt and pepper.

4 Divide the warm borlotti bean balls among bowls and spoon over the soup. Garnish with parsley, parmesan and an extra drizzle of olive oil. ◗

Roasted brussels <u>WITH</u> cauliflower puree <u>AND</u> almonds

1 kg brussels sprouts

80 g butter

1 large onion, diced

1 teaspoon coriander seeds, toasted and ground

400 ml pouring cream

400 g cauliflower, chopped

pinch of grated nutmeg

salt flakes and cracked black pepper

⅔ cup (50 g) coarse breadcrumbs, from day-old white bread

⅓ cup (55 g) roasted almonds, roughly chopped

50 g cheddar, grated

wild rice, to serve

The idea of this dish is to offset some of the brussels sprouts' bitterness with the sweet cauliflower puree. It's not that I don't like the bitterness, but I am aware some people will do anything to avoid a sprout so I will do anything to encourage them to eat one. Anyway, adding a good cheddar to anything makes it taste good. I would enlist in the army if the war was over cheese. It's important stuff. English West Country cheddar is one of my all-time favourites, but we do have some good local aged ones catching up to the Brits' finesse in this area. We have come a very long way in a very short time, and this country is blessed with an amazing bunch of talented, passionate cheesemakers.

The cauli is cooked down in cream much like a classic soubise, which is usually onion-based. While this one does have a touch of onion, most of the flavour comes from the cauliflower and coriander seed (another combination I love). If you can bear to waste the cauli stems, you do get a slightly less stinky puree because the florets are a little cleaner in taste and smell. However, this is something I can never bring myself to do, so I cook the whole lot.

1 Lightly grease a large baking dish. Peel a few outer leaves off the brussels sprouts if they're tatty and choose a few nice leaves for the garnish. Nip the base of the sprout off and cut a cross on the bottom.

2 Boil or steam the sprouts for 6 minutes or until tender, popping the leaves in for the last minute. Arrange the sprouts in the baking dish.

3 Meanwhile, in a large heavy-based saucepan, melt half the butter over low heat. Add the onion and coriander and fry for 5 minutes until the onion is slightly softened. Stir in the cream, cauliflower and nutmeg, then cover and cook for 30 minutes or until the cauliflower is nice and tender. Remove from the heat and use a stick blender to puree the mixture until smooth. Season with salt and pepper, then pour the cauli puree over the brussels sprouts.

4 Preheat the oven to 200°C fan-forced (220°C conventional). Place the breadcrumbs, almonds and cheddar in a bowl, season with salt and pepper, and mix until well combined. Sprinkle the mixture over the brussels sprouts. Bake for 10–15 minutes or until golden.

5 Chuck the reserved sprout leaves on top as garnish and serve with wild rice. ◗

Bamboo, water chestnut AND shiitake stir-fry WITH carrot oil

3 large carrots

1 cup (250 ml) flavour-neutral oil (see page 33)

1 × 550 g tin bamboo shoots, drained and cut into wedges

1 × 300 g tin water chestnuts, drained and halved on an angle

1 teaspoon brown sugar

3 cm young ginger, peeled and sliced into matchsticks

100 g fresh shiitake mushrooms, stems removed, sliced randomly

3 celery sticks, thick ends halved, cut into angled batons

¼ cup (60 ml) vegetarian oyster sauce

⅓ cup (80 ml) light soy sauce

¼ cup (60 ml) shaohsing

steamed jasmine rice, to serve

I love this carrot oil. Not only is it a good way to use up old carrots, but it adds a stunning hue to stir-fry dishes and some complex sweetness to boot. You can buy fresh bamboo shoots at farmers' markets and they are easy to prepare. Simply remove the tough outer leaves and brush off excess dirt, make a deep diagonal incision from head to base (this expedites cooking and also helps with peeling later), and then trim the tough base off. A word of caution, however: bamboo shoots contain a toxin in the form of hydrocyanic acid. A traditional and popular way to make them safe to eat is to chuck ½ cup of rice bran powder per kg of shoots into the cooking water (about 2 litres) – this will neutralise the toxin while the shoots cook. Simmer gently for up to an hour until a skewer passes through the inner flesh with no resistance, then drain and peel the outer layers away until you are left with the fawn-coloured flesh with its amazing little ridges and spear-like appearance.

Or, if you think that is a mad amount of work for a home cook, just buy a tin instead – and next time you order bamboo shoots at a fancy Asian restaurant, you'll appreciate how much work has gone into your dinner when the chef has prepared them fresh for you!

1 Peel two of the carrots, reserving the peel. Slice them in half lengthways, then on an angle into 3 mm thick slices, reserving the trimmings. Set aside. Roughly chop the remaining carrot and place it in a food processor with the reserved peel and trimmings. Blitz to the consistency of rock salt.

2 Transfer the blitzed carrot to a saucepan and add the oil. Bring to a simmer over low heat and cook for 30–40 minutes until the carrot is lightly caramelised and fragrant and the oil is bright orange. Strain the carrot oil through a very fine strainer. You will need 100 ml for the stir-fry; chuck the rest in a bottle and keep it in the fridge for up to 3 months.

3 Heat a wok over high heat and add 100 ml of carrot oil. Add the bamboo shoots and water chestnuts and stir-fry for a minute, then add the sugar and stir-fry until the bamboo is well coloured. Add the ginger, shiitake, celery and sliced carrot and stir-fry briskly – don't lose the crunch in the carrot. Add the oyster sauce, soy sauce and shaohsing. If the wok is hot enough, the oil and the sauces will split rather than emulsify, giving you a vibrant contrast of flavour and colour between the sweet, orange carrot oil and the salty, dark-brown sauces.

4 Divide the stir-fry among bowls and add a little more carrot oil if you like. Serve with steamed rice. ◖

Vietnamese hot pot

90 ml flavour-neutral oil
(see page 33)

2 cloves garlic, chopped

1 tablespoon minced ginger

1 onion, chopped

3 celery sticks, chopped on an
angle into 2 cm pieces

1 large carrot, peeled and chopped
on an angle into 2 cm pieces

100 g fresh shiitake mushrooms,
stems removed, sliced

2 cups (400 g) jasmine rice,
rinsed until the water runs clear

1 × 230 g tin water chestnuts,
drained and halved on an angle

1 teaspoon salt flakes

4 free-range eggs

Crispy shallot chips (see Basics),
to garnish

bean sprouts, to garnish

coriander, to garnish

Sauce

1½ tablespoons light soy sauce

¼ cup (60 ml) kecap manis

¼ cup (60 ml) vegetarian
oyster sauce

3 teaspoons white sugar

1 teaspoon sesame oil

2 spring onions, green parts
only, finely sliced

Packed with an assortment of winter produce, this dish is comforting and substantial enough to perk you up on a winter's night. One-pot wonders are also fantastic motivators for reluctant cooks, being simple to make and quick to wash up. The claypot radiates a very gentle heat and is definitely worth the small investment for the result it delivers.

Coriander can be a little tricky in the warmer months as it is always keen to bolt (which is why I always grow it in the shade). In winter, however, it's generally no trouble and if you have light and sandy soil, it will encourage healthy roots and stems, and robust leaves. I have a particular dislike for flimsy, weedy coriander that just wilts and faints when it leaves the shop. Sure, the leaves are delicate and a little soapy and silky even on the best-grown specimen – but it should not start decomposing as soon as a chef looks its way and merely threatens to cook it. I think that's why so many people hate this herb with a passion: they have just had a badly grown example. So if your coriander is even slightly mushy or slimy, don't go there. It is the real hero of this dish and it needs to be shining with freshness.

1 For the sauce, place all the ingredients in a small bowl and stir until well combined. Set aside.

2 In a claypot or casserole over low heat, heat ¼ cup (60 ml) of the oil and saute the garlic, ginger, onion, celery, carrot and shiitakes for 3–4 minutes. Add the rice, water chestnuts and salt and saute for a couple of minutes, then add cold water to reach 2–3 cm above the rice. Bring to the boil, then reduce the heat to low. Cover with the lid and simmer for 15 minutes until the rice has absorbed all the liquid.

3 Preheat the oven to 180°C fan-forced (200°C conventional). Stir half the sauce gently through the rice. Cover with the lid and place the claypot or casserole in the oven for 20 minutes.

4 Meanwhile, add the remaining oil to a frying pan over low heat. Crack the eggs in, then cover with a lid and fry very gently until the whites are set but the yolks are still runny.

5 To serve, spoon the rice into bowls and top with a fried egg. Garnish with crispy shallots, bean sprouts and coriander, and serve with the remaining sauce on the side. ◗

Serves 4

Braised celery hearts WITH green olives, white beans AND romesco

1 cup (200 g) butter (lima) beans, soaked overnight in cold water

1½ tablespoons extra virgin olive oil

salt flakes and cracked black pepper

200 g butter

½ cup (60 g) green olives

2 decent-sized or 4 small celery hearts

100 ml dry white wine

¼ teaspoon dried Greek oregano

1 cup (260 g) Romesco sauce (see Basics)

marjoram leaves, to garnish

flat-leaf parsley leaves, to garnish

You don't need young celery to get a celery heart. I actually think older celery is better, so this dish is perfect for winter when big, chunky bunches are available. Simply keep peeling back the outer sticks until you reach the tightly wound, paler bunch with baby leaves. These are sweet and anise-y and have none of the stringiness of the outer stalks.

I know the amount of butter required to braise the hearts here is outrageous but I always just freeze it afterwards and use it with other vegies, as it retains a lovely aniseed flavour. Frying the olives and celery at the end of cooking turns the otherwise pale flavours into something a little more robust, which is needed to compete with the big smoky–sweetness of the romesco sauce.

1 Drain and rinse the beans, then place them in a saucepan with 3 cups (750 ml) of water and the olive oil. Simmer over medium heat for about 45 minutes or until tender. Drain, then season with salt and pepper.

2 Preheat the oven to 180°C fan-forced (200°C conventional). While the beans are cooking, place the butter in a small (about 1 litre) ovenproof dish on the stovetop over low heat. Heat until the butter fizzes up a little, then add the olives, celery hearts, wine and oregano. Season with salt. Add up to ½ cup (125 ml) of water to cover the celery hearts, then pop the dish in the oven and cook for about 15 minutes until the celery hearts are tender but still intact. Remove the celery and olives with a slotted spoon and gently cut the hearts in half lengthways (or leave whole if they are small).

3 Heat a frying pan over medium heat and add the braised celery hearts and olives; the residual butter will caramelise them in just a few seconds, so jiggle the pan and turn the celery to ensure even colouring. Remove from the heat and set aside.

4 Warm the romesco sauce in a small saucepan over low heat. Spoon the beans onto plates and top with the romesco, celery hearts and olives. Garnish with marjoram and parsley. ◗

Beancurd rolls

20 g dried shiitake mushrooms

2 tablespoons cornflour mixed with 2 tablespoons water

½ teaspoon sichuan peppercorns

10 g crumbly beancurd (see Ingredients)

1 tablespoon dark soy sauce

2 tablespoons Chinese light soy sauce (see page 85)

120 ml peanut oil

1 teaspoon white sugar

2 purple carrots, peeled and cut into matchsticks

200 g bean sprouts

2 tablespoons shaohsing

big pinch of cracked white pepper

2 large salted beancurd sheets (see Ingredients)

1 lemon, cut into wedges

A big acknowledgement to Cheong Liew for this one. I never cooked this dish when I was on his watch, but we ate it at a local Chinese restaurant one time and Cheong talked me through it. It's this generosity that makes working in my industry a pleasure. Chefs who mentor, encourage and teach should not be undervalued. I feel the true distinction of a great chef is the trail of great chefs he leaves behind and Cheong has many little 'Liews' all over the world now making their own mark. The crumbly beancurd pieces in these rolls suck up all the flavours and their delicate texture works brilliantly alongside the chewy shiitakes and crunchy purple carrots.

1 Soak the shiitake mushrooms in 1.5 litres of water for 1 hour. Cut off the stems and discard them, then thinly slice the caps. Strain the soaking water into a saucepan and boil for 5–10 minutes until reduced to ½ cup (125 ml). Remove the pan from the heat and stream in the cornflour mixture, whisking continuously to thicken.

2 Place the sichuan peppercorns in a dry frying pan over low heat and gently toast until highly aromatic, tossing regularly to prevent burning. (If the peppercorns turn dark brown or smoke excessively, they will become bitter, so err on the side of caution.) Leave the peppercorns to cool for 5 minutes, then grind in a spice grinder or pound quite finely – but not to dust! – using a mortar and pestle.

3 Place the crumbly beancurd in a small bowl and splash with the dark soy, 1 tablespoon of light soy, 1 tablespoon of peanut oil and 2 tablespoons of the shiitake water. Toss around and allow the beancurd to soften up a little and macerate.

4 Heat ¼ cup (60 ml) of peanut oil in a frying pan over high heat and fry the sliced shiitakes until brown and slightly crispy, then add the sugar. Add the carrot and cook for a few minutes until tender, then add the bean sprouts and crumbly beancurd, along with any marinade left in the bowl, and toss together. Add the shaohsing, pepper and remaining light soy and stir-fry together. Check the seasoning, adding a little more light soy or salt if required.

5 Remove the pan from the heat and stir in about ¼ cup (60 ml) of the shiitake water until everything binds. Return the pan to low heat and cook for 30 seconds or so until the mixture clumps together a little. Transfer the filling mixture to a bowl and set aside.

Beancurd rolls *(cont.)*

6 Set a large steamer on a saucepan of water over medium–high heat. Unfold the beancurd sheets, spraying them with a little water to soften if necessary. Brush both sides with the remaining shiitake water. Place half the filling mixture along one edge and roll up to enclose. Repeat with the remainign beancurd sheet and filling. Lightly oil the steamer tray and place the beancurd rolls inside, seam-side down. Steam with the lid on for 10 minutes. The skin should hold the filling, but will remain quite fragile and wrinkly.

7 It's a good idea to cool the rolls in the fridge for an hour; this will allow them to set, which makes for easier frying.

8 Place the remaining peanut oil in a frying pan over medium heat. Fry the beancurd rolls for a minute or so on each side until browned and crispy.

9 To serve, cut the rolls on an angle into 2.5 cm slices. Serve with lemon wedges and a sprinkle of sichuan pepper. ◑

Roast potatoes WITH nettles AND horseradish yoghurt

1 kg waxy potatoes (such as kipflers or bintjes)

50 g butter, melted

½ cup (125 ml) olive oil

¼ cup (60 ml) lemon juice

1 teaspoon dried Greek oregano

salt flakes and cracked
black pepper

2 cloves garlic, crushed

100 g nettles, picked
(or baby spinach)

¼ cup (60 ml) verjuice

¼ cup (70 g) Greek-style yoghurt

2 teaspoons freshly
grated horseradish

Allow me a small grumble. Everyone is slinging around the word 'foraged' on their menus. Fine and trendy, yes, but the fact is this is just a part of cooking! Cultures have procured food one way or another for centuries. They either grew it, gathered it, traded it or were given it because someone cared about them. So 'foraged' is a redundant menu term in my opinion. After all, you wouldn't say 'shopped waxy potato' or 'ordered-over-the-phone horseradish', would you? I guess the aim of saying 'foraged' is to imply the chef has put in some effort; I suppose it could also imply there was some care along the way. But I am more interested in where it came from, how it was grown and who is getting the money if it was traded, rather than how it has been collected when it's ready to eat. I think when we started treating food as a commodity we forgot some of this.

Okay, got that off my chest. Nettles are everywhere in winter so indulge in an act of freeganism and grab some. They are fans of cracks in the footpath and carparks (and around my wheelie bins at home). Always pick the leaves before they go to flower or seed, and don't forget to wear a couple of pairs of kitchen gloves, or you will be foraging for some calamine lotion.

1 Place the spuds in a large saucepan and cover with cold salted water. Bring to the boil over high heat and cook for about 10 minutes or until just starting to become tender. Remove from the heat and drain, then cut the spuds into wedges.

2 Preheat the oven to 200°C fan-forced (220°C conventional). Combine the butter, 2 tablespoons of olive oil and 2 tablespoons of lemon juice in a jug and whisk together. Place the potato wedges in a roasting tin and use a spoon to gently crush them in places. Brush the potatoes with the butter and lemon mixture and season them generously with oregano, salt and pepper. Roast for 30 minutes until really crispy and golden.

3 Meanwhile, fry the remaining olive oil and garlic in a frying pan over medium heat for 2 minutes, then add the nettles or spinach and verjuice and cook for 2–3 minutes until wilted. Season with salt and pepper.

4 Combine the yoghurt, horseradish and remaining lemon juice, stirring until well combined. Season to taste.

5 To serve, arrange the roast potatoes on a plate, scatter over the nettles and drizzle with horseradish yoghurt. ◗

Over-roasted Asian mushrooms WITH crispy seaweed AND noodles

280 g soba noodles

45 ml peanut oil

100 g oyster mushrooms, ripped into wedges

100 g enoki mushrooms, trimmed

100 g king brown mushrooms, finely sliced

100 g shimeji mushrooms, trimmed

25 g dried wakame
or 120 g fresh wakame
(see Ingredients)

½ teaspoon togarashi seven spice

Dipping sauce

¼ cup (60 ml) mirin

squeeze of lemon juice
(or 2 teaspoons yuzu)

1 tablespoon white sugar

100 ml light soy sauce

2 spring onions, green parts only, finely sliced

It seems wrong to over-roast delicate Asian mushrooms, but it really is a great method. The resulting dish is intensely flavoured and wintry, yet light at the same time. The mushrooms end up all crispy and the paper-thin wakame disintegrates almost as it hits your mouth. Don't get too bogged down with finding the exact combination of mushrooms here. Just get a variety of textures from dainty to robust, as this brings more interest to the final dish. The togarashi seven spice is easy to find in Japanese supermarkets, as are the soba noodles. Make sure you rinse the noodles under warm water after cooking, as this prevents them from clumping together in a mess when you serve them.

1 Preheat the oven to 180°C fan-forced (200°C conventional).

2 Cook the soba noodles for 5 minutes in a saucepan of rapidly boiling salted water. Drain the noodles and run them under warm water, then drain them again. Toss in a teaspoon of peanut oil and set aside (you'll be serving them at room temperature).

3 Place all the mushrooms on a baking tray, add 1 tablespoon of peanut oil and mix well to coat. Place the wakame on another baking tray and coat with the remaining peanut oil. Roast for 20 minutes or until the mushrooms and wakame are crispy.

4 For the dipping sauce, place the mirin and lemon juice or yuzu in a bowl, add the sugar and whisk to dissolve. Add the soy sauce, spring onion and 300 ml of water and stir to combine.

5 Arrange the noodles, mushrooms and wakame on a serving plate and sprinkle with togarashi. Serve the dipping sauce in a bowl on the side. Dip the noodles in the sauce as you go or, if you are using a noodle mat, pour a little of the sauce over the top as the surplus will simply drain through. ◗

Stilton, parsnip and potato pasties

1 free-range egg, lightly beaten
with a pinch of salt

Pastry

500 g strong bread flour

2 teaspoons salt flakes

⅓ cup (80 g) virgin coconut oil

Filling

60 g butter

500 g waxy potatoes
(such as kipflers or bintjes),
peeled and diced

500 g parsnip, peeled and diced

300 g swede, peeled and diced

1 large leek, washed,
halved and finely sliced

salt flakes and cracked
black pepper

100 g stilton, crumbled

handful of dill leaves,
roughly chopped

large handful of flat-leaf parsley
leaves, roughly chopped

It can be tricky to make a good vegetarian pasty dough without the traditional lard or suet, but my secret is to use coconut oil to achieve a similar mouthfeel. Coconut oil also remains firm at higher temperatures and this makes the dough lush, pliable and robust. What's more, apart from palm oil (which I personally avoid for health and ethical reasons), it is the only saturated veg oil and if you are vegan or vego you might be missing the small quantities from your diet that are essential to health.

A vegie pasty can also be let down by its filling (minced up carrots et al, yawn) but I'm happy to say that after years of messing around with this recipe, I have discovered the winning combination – stilton, swede, parsnip, potato and leek. The egg wash at the end is not essential, but I think shortcrust pastry can look a little sad without the gloss that it brings. Feel free to omit and go 'dull' though: you will gain a little more flakiness on the outside casing.

1 For the pastry, combine the flour and salt in a bowl and lightly rub in the coconut oil until the mixture resembles breadcrumbs. Add ⅓ cup (80 ml) of cold water, then transfer to a food processor and pulse until the pastry comes together. (If you want a firmer dough you can pulse a little longer, but I like this dough flaky.) Wrap the dough in plastic film and leave in the fridge for 3 hours.

2 For the filling, melt the butter in a large saute or frying pan over medium heat. Add the potato, parsnip, swede and leek and season with salt and pepper. Saute for 8–10 minutes until tender, then turn the veg onto a tray and place in the fridge to chill for 20 minutes. Transfer the chilled veg to a bowl and fold in the stilton and herbs.

3 Preheat the oven to 180°C fan-forced (200°C conventional) and line two baking trays with baking paper. Divide the dough into four and roll on a lightly floured benchtop until 5 mm thick. Place a quarter of the filling in the centre of each round and bring the pastry up around it, crimping the edges together to seal. (The dough can become soft and unmanageable quite quickly if your room and hands are too warm; you may need to re-chill it for a few minutes if this is the case.)

4 Place the pasties on the prepared baking trays and brush with egg. Bake for 25–30 minutes or until the pastry is golden. ◑

Pumpkin, chickpea AND tahini soup

1½ cups (300 g) dried kabuli chickpeas (see Ingredients), soaked overnight in cold water

1 teaspoon smoked paprika

⅓ cup (80 ml) olive oil

salt flakes and cracked black pepper

1 kg pumpkin, peeled, seeded and chopped

2 teaspoons ras el hanout

1 onion, chopped

¼ cup (70 g) tahini

¼ cup (60 ml) lemon juice

1 teaspoon finely grated lemon zest

small handful of flat-leaf parsley, chopped

Pumpkin and soup are two words that together usually make me run from the kitchen. It's not that I don't like soup, or pumpkin, but quite often when the two collide the result is so inoffensive that it is – um, how to be polite here? – beige food. Having said that, we all have those nights when we clean out the fridge and pantry and surprise ourselves with the resulting dish. This one came about because I always have tahini and a good stock of spices, and I always cook extra chickpeas when they are called for in a recipe and freeze them in a takeaway container. Add some almost-on-the-turn veg and I am pleased to say I now like pumpkin soup.

This recipe works because the tahini and chickpeas push all the sweet pumpkin flavours to a more grounded, grown-up and earthy place, and the baked chickpeas are a welcome textural variance to the smooth puree. The spice mix ras el hanout varies wildly from blend to blend but it always carries with its aroma an exotic and dreamy image of faraway bustling markets . . . and I haven't even been to North Africa: it's just a thing that happens when I smell it!

1 Preheat the oven to 180°C fan-forced (200°C conventional) and line two baking trays with baking paper. Place a third of the chickpeas on one tray and sprinkle with paprika and 1 tablespoon of olive oil. Season with salt and toss until the chickpeas are well coated. Roast for 25 minutes or until the chickpeas are crispy. Set aside.

2 Meanwhile, place the pumpkin in a bowl and add 2 tablespoons of olive oil and the ras el hanout. Season with salt. Transfer to the baking tray and roast for 30 minutes or until the pumpkin is tender and a little coloured, then set aside.

3 Heat the remaining olive oil in a large heavy-based saucepan over low heat. Add the onion and saute until glassy, then add the remaining chickpeas and 2 litres of water. Increase the heat to medium and bring to the boil, then reduce to a simmer, cover and cook for 40 minutes or until the chickpeas are tender. Add the pumpkin to the saucepan and warm everything through, then whizz it all up with a stick blender, adding water if the soup is too thick. Season to taste.

4 Spoon the soup into bowls. Whisk the tahini and lemon juice with a tablespoon of warm water to form a paste. Drizzle the lemon tahini over the soup and sprinkle with lemon zest, parsley and black pepper. Garnish with the crispy chickpeas and serve. ◗

Pear crostata
with muscatels

¼ cup (60 ml) verjuice

handful of roasted almonds,
roughly chopped

mint sprigs, to garnish

Pastry

130 g plain flour, sifted

¼ cup (40 g) wholemeal flour,
sifted

50 g almond meal

80 g caster sugar

1 teaspoon finely grated lemon zest

pinch of salt flakes

100 g cold unsalted butter,
cut into small pieces

1 free-range egg, plus 1 free-range
egg yolk, lightly beaten

Filling

5 large pears, cut into wedges
(about 12 per pear)

100 g unsalted butter, chopped

½ cup (110 g) dark brown sugar

finely grated zest and juice
of ½ lemon

good pinch of saffron threads

¼ cup (60 ml) sherry

1 cup (160 g) muscatels

A crostata is a tart without a tart tin. I am a little 'baking-challenged' or, as some of the chefs I work with are keen to point out, I am a little special to watch when it comes to using sugar and scales. I'm a hot-handed little beast as well, which doesn't help: most tart doughs turn to silly putty when I wave at them from a distance. Therefore, a freeform tart where a rustic appearance is considered desirable is something I'm more comfortable with than rows of delicate, intricate tartlets.

The pears are your choice here. I like using 'cookers' or the soft-fleshed ones and letting them turn to mush because the dough is crunchy enough to still give the dish some structure. My favourite dark sugar remains Billington's molasses, but I am trying to wean myself off imports. Luckily, Australian dark brown sugar has a nice fudginess and brings a moist caramel to the finished dish.

1 For the pastry, combine the flours with the almond meal, sugar, lemon zest and salt in a large bowl, stirring until well combined. Rub the butter into the flour mixture until it resembles breadcrumbs. Add the egg and yolk, mixing until the dough just comes together. Flatten out the dough slightly, then wrap it in plastic film and chill in the fridge for at least 2 hours.

2 Preheat the oven to 200°C fan-forced (220°C conventional) and line a baking tray with baking paper. For the filling, toss the pears in a bowl with the butter, sugar, lemon juice, saffron and sherry. Transfer to the prepared tray and roast for 30 minutes. Strain off the cooking juices and reserve. Set the pears aside to cool.

3 Turn down the oven to 190°C fan-forced (210°C conventional) and line a baking tray with baking paper. Remove the dough from the fridge and leave it at room temperature for 15 minutes. On a lightly floured benchtop, roll it into a 26 cm round, then carefully transfer it to the prepared tray. Place the cooled roast pears, lemon zest and muscatels in the centre, leaving a 5 cm border. Roughly fold and crimp up the edges to encase the filling. Bake for 30 minutes or until the pastry is set.

4 Meanwhile, place the reserved pear juices in a small saucepan over medium heat and add the verjuice. Reduce for about 10 minutes until thick and syrupy, turning down the heat towards the end to ensure the syrup doesn't burn. Set aside to cool.

5 Allow the tart to cool slightly before serving. Drizzle over the pear syrup and garnish with chopped almonds and mint. ●

BASICS

Romesco sauce

½ head garlic, halved

2 large ripe tomatoes, halved

4 large red capsicums (peppers)

½ cup (125 ml) extra virgin olive oil, plus extra to seal the jar

50 g stale white bread (such as ciabatta), ripped into 3 cm pieces

100 g almonds

1 tablespoon red wine vinegar

½ teaspoon sweet smoked paprika

1 teaspoon salt flakes

½ teaspoon cracked black pepper

When the first ripe capsicums of the season appear, I just want to enjoy them fresh in a salad or stir-fry. Nearer the end of summer though, gluts abound and this is nature's way of saying: Put 'em in a jar! Making a lot of something really doesn't take much longer than making a little and there is great satisfaction in having a pantry lined with jars of sauces and pickles. We are all squirrels at heart.

When people talk about food security, I nod my head attentively but I can't help thinking more about pantry insecurity! We live in a world in which a few big players control the lion's share of retail food supply and, let's face it, we don't really know who they are. We sit on a couple of day's worth of supplies at home and whip up to the supermarket whenever we need something, assuming what we want will be waiting there for us. Or do we? I think there is a little bit of devolutionary worry buried inside us, a little guy who is terrified the shelves won't be stacked with food. Until a hundred years ago, preserving was an absolute necessity. In my grandparents' day it was about sensible home economics but also, perhaps more importantly, it was a way of feeling safe and in control. These days I know it's tokenistic – after all, a few bottles of romesco sauce are not going to see me through a food disaster – but after a day of ramming stuff in jars, I just feel better and that's got to be worth something. This is a pantry staple of mine and it makes a delicious pasta sauce and dip; you can also use it in the Braised celery heart recipe on page 213.

1 Preheat the oven to 210°C fan-forced (230°C conventional).

2 Place the garlic, tomatoes and capsicums on a large baking tray, and drizzle with half the olive oil. Roast for 30 minutes, then remove the garlic and set it aside. Roast the tomatoes and capsicums for a further 10 minutes or until they begin to blister and colour.

3 Meanwhile, heat the remaining olive oil in a heavy-based frying pan over medium heat. Add the bread and almonds and fry about a minute, stirring often, until the bread is crispy and golden – the almonds will also be a shade or so darker by this time. Remove from the pan and set aside.

4 Place the roast capsicums in a bowl, cover with plastic film and leave to sweat for 10 minutes, then peel the skins and remove the seeds and stems. Squeeze the roasted garlic cloves out of their skin.

5 Place the garlic, capsicum and tomato in a food processor together with the breadcrumbs and almonds, vinegar, paprika, salt and pepper. Blitz until smooth.

6 Pour the romesco sauce into a 1 litre sterilised jar and seal with a layer of olive oil. It will keep for up to 3 months in the fridge. ◕

Pickled bean sprouts

100 g bean sprouts

2 teaspoons white sugar

1 teaspoon salt flakes

1 tablespoon rice vinegar

1 large red chilli, thinly sliced

Quick pickling is a useful way of preserving and – let's face it – how many times have you thrown out bean sprouts because they were looking brown and sad? These are particularly good with the Stir-fried cucumber on page 53, but will add an interesting texture to almost any stir-fry.

1 Combine the bean sprouts, sugar and salt in a small bowl and leave to stand for 1 hour, turning occasionally.

2 Tip out the tablespoon or so of liquid that has pooled in the bowl and very gently squeeze the bean sprouts, then return them to the bowl with the rice vinegar and chilli and mix to combine. ◖

Fills a 200 ml jar

Crispy shallot chips

4–6 golden shallots, finely sliced

600 ml flavour-neutral oil
(see page 33)

salt flakes

Crispy shallot chips are great but most bought ones contain partially hydrolysed palm oil to make them super-crispy and shelf-stable. Make your own and they stay crispy for a week or so if you follow the method of gently converting the sugars by starting in cold oil. The salt then helps keep them crispy by drawing any residual moisture during storage. The bottom line is most food additives are put in food to obtain an unrealistic shelf life or to achieve a hyper flavour that I think only tastes fake. Give 'em a skip and make it from scratch where possible.

1 Place the shallots in a small–medium saucepan and cover with the oil. Place over low heat and leave to heat up gently; this allows the sugars to convert slowly, which makes the shallots really sweet and crispy without burning. Simmer the shallots in the oil, without disturbing them. They will foam until the moisture evaporates, and then after about 10 minutes the pan will become quiet; from this point the shallots can turn from golden to burnt in just a couple of minutes, so stand by . . . When the shallots are just golden, remove them with a spider or slotted spoon and drain on paper towel. Immediately sprinkle well with salt, as this will help draw out excess oil. Leave to cool. Store the crispy shallot chips in an airtight jar for up to a year. You can also keep the oil for stir-frying – it has a great sweet onion flavour. ◖

Mushroom paste

½ cup (20 g) dried porcini

⅓ cup (80 ml) extra virgin olive oil, plus extra to cover

3 golden shallots, diced

3 sprigs oregano, leaves picked

3 sprigs thyme, leaves picked

3 cloves garlic, finely chopped

500 g assorted mushrooms (portobellos, swiss brown, shiitakes with stems removed, field mushrooms, whatever you can lay your hands on)

1 tablespoon salt flakes

½ cup (125 ml) dry white wine

2½ tablespoons red wine vinegar

This is bit of a go-to in my kitchen, born out of an intense dislike of the chemical taste of artifical truffle pastes. I thought I'd have a shot at making my own version and I'm pleased to report it was a resounding success. Now I always have a jar of this on standby for tossing through warm pasta, folding into risotto at the end of cooking, spreading over bruschetta, smearing over asparagus spears and adding to frittata or quiches. It's also used in the Pie floater on page 39 and the Artichoke stacciare on page 57.

1 Place the porcini in a bowl and pour over the warm water until the porcini are just covered. (Make sure you use only the minimum amount of water required to cover, otherwise you'll be reducing the paste for a long time later in the recipe!) Soak the porcini for 20 minutes or until soft, then strain them through a fine sieve, squeezing the juice from the porcini and reserving the soaking liquid. Finely chop the porcini.

2 In a large sauteuse or frying pan, heat the olive oil over medium heat, then add the shallot and fry until fragrant. Add the chopped porcini and stir. Add the herbs and garlic, continuing to stir. Add all the mushrooms and saute for about 10–15 minutes – it can take quite a lot of time for the mushrooms to really cook out. A good indicator is the oil in the pan: at first the mushrooms act like sponges and suck up all the oil, but once they're cooked, they start to give the oil back. They also become highly aromatic. When the mushrooms are cooked, add the salt. Deglaze the pan with the wine and then the vinegar and continue to cook until the liquid has evaporated. Add the reserved porcini liquid and simmer until it has evaporated.

3 Remove the pan from the heat and blend the mushroom mixture with a stick blender; you want it to retain a little texture, a bit like crunchy peanut butter. Store in a sterilised jar in the fridge for up to 3 months. ●

Shiitake stock

1 cup (30 g) dried
shiitake mushrooms

1.6 litres cold water

2 cm ginger, bruised

2 spring onions

Shiitakes are the big-flavour daddy of Asian mushrooms, much as porcini are to French and Italian cooking. If you're concerned some of your vegie cooking is lacking punch, this simple stock is sure to ramp it up . . .

1 Place the shiitakes in a large saucepan and add the water. Leave them to soak for a couple of hours.

2 Add the ginger and spring onions (folded up to fit) to the saucepan, then bring to a gentle simmer over medium heat. Simmer for 1 hour, then strain through a muslin-lined sieve, pressing lightly with the back of a ladle to extract as much liquid as possible without mangling the mushrooms.

3 The stock can be kept for 1 week in an airtight container in the fridge or frozen for up to 6 months. The drained shiitakes will keep for 1 week in an airtight container in the fridge. ◖

Makes 300 g

Egg yolk mayo

3 free-range egg yolks

1 tablespoon dijon mustard

200 ml olive oil

¼ cup (60 ml) lemon juice

salt flakes and cracked
black pepper

1 tablespoon boiling water

Bought mayonnaise is usually just a horrible emulsion of (often bad) oil and water and some chemicals . . . Eek. This version is easy to make and you can squirrel it away in a sterilised jar in the fridge for up to a week.

1 Combine the egg yolks in a food processor, then add the mustard. With the motor still running, very slowly drizzle in the olive oil until you have a lovely, thick emulsion; be careful not to add the oil too quickly or the mayo will split. Add the lemon juice, then salt and pepper to taste. Finally add a tablespoon of boiling water to stabilise the lot. ◖

ACKNOWLEDGEMENTS

'Nothing is original. Steal from anywhere that resonates with inspiration or fuels your imagination.' Jim Jarmusch

There is a legion of people behind this book, I am not exaggerating. Everything I know about cooking and food is part of a collective knowledge that I am just lucky enough to belong to. It's called culture. Some conveyed this knowledge by cooking with their progeny, some exchanged it through storytelling, some wrote it down. When I cook something, it's this collective noise – everything I have been taught, everything I have seen, heard and read about – that fuels my creativity. So, to that cast of thousands, thank you.

More specifically, to my cohorts closer to hand, because it is their gentle nudges, hard grind, inspiration and support that I am most in debt and thankful for:

Fiona Roberts, for cooking on the computer. She knows the difference between a spoon and a cup (I don't): without her drafting, literally nothing would add up!

Blanky and Jodes, for the shopping, chopping, recipe testing, ripping food out of your own vegie patches, smudges of pencil over oil-splattered test sheets, and for reminding me to breathe and drink water during shoots.

Alan Benson, what can I say? You ever so quietly go about your craft, making the light play in ways that bring a plate of food to life. You are a photographic sorcerer.

Ariane Durkin, because a great editor is to a writer what good ingredients are to a chef. Without either I would be well and truly stuffed, and both make me appear better than I am.

And, on that note, thanks for the produce for my plates and for this book in particular: Rachel McMillan from Scoop, Margy and Chris (Carol) from AMJ Produce, Pat and Lina from Patlin Gardens, Simorne from the

236

Organic and Sustainable Market, Bill from House of Organics, Barry from Beach Organics, Ulli from B.-d Farm Paris Creek, Kris from Woodside Cheese Wrights, the boys (and their cow girls) from Fleuriue Milk, Jon from Cleland Gully Eggs, Chester from House of Health for the good stuff, and too many other suppliers for their endless support and dedication.

Carlo Jensen, for the style. You came with your funny little car filled with plates, cutlery, cloth and kibble and gave us a wonderful stage to play on.

Thank you also to those who influence from a little further afield, but nonetheless are there every step of the way:

Lantern designers Alissa Dinallo and Evi O, for making a bunch of random pics and texts into a book. How this happens is probably witchcraft because the result is spectacular.

On that note, Rachel Carter and Pam Dunne for proofreading. Thanks for your sharp eyes.

Chief of the Lanterns, Julie Gibbs, for letting me give birth to a second book even though the first one came out kicking and screaming. I have no idea how you get a bunch of unruly chefs to produce such stunning books. I suspect you can herd cats.

Fellow Tasting Australia creative people, Paul 'Wine Hero' Henry and Maggie Beer. I am privileged to be able to call you friends, and indebted for the waves of inspiration that radiate just from a chat. If ever I feel secretly ready to hang up my clogs and run away to join the circus, five minutes in your company makes me go home and pop them back on.

And now just sit down, *don't* shut up and eat.

INDEX

LANTERN

UK | USA | Canada | Ireland | Australia
India | New Zealand | South Africa | China

Penguin Books is part of the Penguin Random House group of companies
whose addresses can be found at global.penguinrandomhouse.com.

First published by Penguin Group (Australia), 2015

10 9 8 7 6 5 4 3 2 1

Cover design and text layout by Alissa Dinallo © Penguin Group (Australia)
Initial design by Evi O
Cover photograph by Alan Benson
Food styling by Carlo Jensen

Typeset in Eames Century Modern by Post Pre-Press Group, Brisbane, Queensland
Colour separation by Splitting Image Colour Studio, Clayton, Victoria
Printed and bound in China by Printed in China by 1010 Printing International Limited

National Library of Australia
Cataloguing-in-Publication data:

Bryant, Simon

Vegetables, grains and other good stuff

ISBN: 9781921383861 (paperback)

Includes index.

Vegetarian cooking.
Cooking (Vegetables)

Benson, Alan, photographer

641.5636

penguin.com.au/lantern